ex libris

# Fit for a Queen

## ⇒ A Recipe Book ⇐

RESEARCHED FROM
THE HANDWRITTEN
MANUSCRIPTS

*of*

## Ada Parsons

1888 - 1958

### HEAD COOK
*to*
### The Earl *of* Strathmore

c1912 - 1916

Researched and written

by

Jane Joseph
*Grand daughter*

and

Guy Poltock
*Grandson*

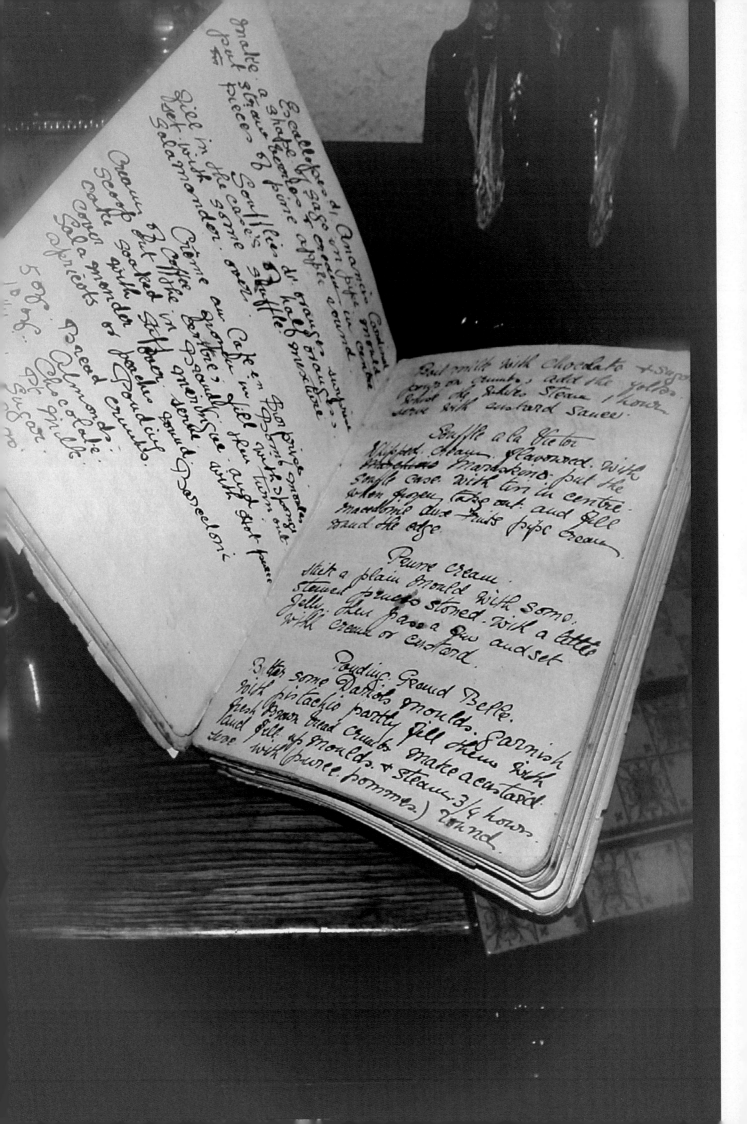

*(Left page — rotated handwriting)*

Bnoll brevad, Apricots. Custard...
a shake boiled Sage... on top in case
put sliced piece of pears. apple round
pieces. Soufflées Puff...
fill in the case some Soufflé
put with some Shelf
Salamander. over.

Crème au Café en Surprise
Coffee Soufflé in Bottle, fill them turn out
Coffee soaked in Bottle, gradually fill then turn out
Cases with Almonds. send round with stock sauce
Creamy but mould or peaches round Pudding
Scoop soaked in... 
Cover mould or peaches. round Macaroni.
Sala mander with
apricots.

Bread Pudding
5 oz. Almonds.
10 oz. Chocolate.
do milk. do milk.
do Sugar.
do

*(Right page)*

Put milk with Chocolate + Sugar
over on crumbs. add the yolks
Scald dry gelatin. Steam 1 hour
serve with custard sauce.

Soufflé à la Victor
Whipped cream flavoured with
Maraschino Maraskino. put the
Soufflé case with tin in centre.
when frozen take out. and fill
macaroni aux fruits pipe cream
round the edge.

Prune cream.
Stick a plain mould with some
stewed prunes stoned. with a little
Jelly. then pour a few and set
with cream or custard.

Pudding. Ground Belle.
Butter some Dariole moulds. Garnish
with pistachio partly fill them with
fresh brown bread crumbs. make a custard
and fill up moulds. + steam 3/4 hours
serve with puree. (pommes.) round.

# Dedication

*This book is dedicated to the memory of*
*Ada and her husband Frank Mattin,*
*and their children*
*Lorna, John and Zena*

## Acknowledgements

In conducting the research for this book we wish to thank The Right Honourable Sir Simon Bowes Lyon, the Earl of Strathmore and the Bowes Lyon Family for their assistance with information and kind encouragement to proceed with this publication. We are also very grateful to Ingrid Thompson, archivist of the Estate records at Glamis Castle for her invaluable efforts to seek out additional information and point us in the right direction to find other sources.

We are indebted to Mr Martin Allan, Archives Assistant at the Highland Archive and Registration Centre, Inverness for answering our questions and searching out important documents for us.

We would also like to thank Mr Robin Rhoderick-Jones and Mr Tom Jaine for their kind help and advice in the final stages of the manuscript.

Also thanks to Antony Garrett Game Dealer *(www.gamedealers.net)* for his help in providing game for the picture on page 21.

The authors

First Edition 2011

Published & Printed by Cranfield Press

## *The authors*

Jane Joseph, granddaughter of Ada Parsons studied Medieval and Modern History as graduate and postgraduate at the London School of Economics under the tutelage of Dr David Starkey, Dr John Gillingham and Dr Antony Bridbury in the late 1970s. She then taught history and humanities in secondary schools in the United Kingdom and Dubai until 1991 when she migrated with her Guyanese husband to Guyana, South America and together, set up their own private charity school for the children of poor villagers in her husband's birth village. Wherever she has taught, her dedication to family and social history has driven her work and motivated her to set up school and local museums in order to keep children in touch with the history of their ancestors. Following the sudden death of both her parents and life threatening medical condition developed by her husband, she was forced to return to England and sadly, for want of suitable successors to continue it, to close down the charity school. Since her return she has become a freelance writer and historian who together with her brother, graphic designer, Guy Poltock, decided jointly to publish these unique historical manuscripts preserved in their family for three generations. This collection of recipes accompanied by a brief social history and biography shows a picture of royalty from the rarely documented viewpoint of a lowly born servant.

# Contents

*Ada and Frank Mattin's children Lorna, John and Zena with Janet and Harry Knight and their family on Knight's farm East Hall, St Paul's Walden next to the Strathmore Estate in the late 1920s. They had been catching rabbits at harvest time. According to the Ground Game Act passed by Gladstone's ministry in 1880, farmers could legally shoot rabbits and hares and other ground game on their own property in the daytime without a licence, since these were damaging farmers' crops.*

# Introduction

The original manuscript for the recipes in this book is in the form of a personal notebook kept by Ada for use in the kitchen in the households in which she served. They are all in her own handwriting apart from a few loose papers signed "Lady Cavendish" and which therefore may have been "her ladyship's" (*The Countess of Strathmore's*) writing passed to Ada to follow. However, some of the recipes elsewhere in the book are annotated "Miss Bullen's Receipt" or "Mrs Hughes Receipt" and which were obviously passed on to Ada during her time working with Alice Hughes at the Marquis of Winchester's House, Amport St Mary, or when she was at Lockerley Hall, and written in Ada's own hand.

Ada had only a basic primary education, before beginning work as a maid or trainee cook, and the recipes were not organised in date order in the hard bound notebook. She appears to have added to it throughout the years, as there is evidence of progression and of some instruction from a more senior cook. In the first few pages, she has comments such as "fine" written under the recipe. This seems as if someone checked her work and marked it, although it could be her own comment as to whether the recipe worked well in practice after she had tried it out.

On another early page, she has listed all the dishes she knew that could be made from apples as if this were an exercise set for her to do. The first recipes which seem to have been recorded were for simple dishes such as croutes or canapés and biscuits or cakes. Some of them also give specific instructions as to which piece of equipment to use, such as "use the egg bowl", or "in the sauté pan" indicating a novice taking down instructions received in the kitchen.

This is not to suggest that Ada was a complete beginner in the kitchen when she first went out to service at the age of fourteen. Her mother would definitely have taught Ada the basics at home, enabling this, her eldest daughter to help in the preparation of family meals even before she went to primary school. Nothing less was expected of a girl in that era. Not only would she have wanted to copy and learn to do what her mother did, but also there would have been a need for her to learn and pass on to her younger female siblings those basic life skills if their mother was out working to earn an income. Even if she remained at home, a mother would need all the help she could get to prepare family meals and keep the house clean, especially when she had to nurse infants, hand make clothing for the family or do the laborious home preparation of preserves. The female role in life was still expected to be domestic, whether at home or in the employ of wealthier folk in their neighbourhood, as it had been from the earliest times.

In any case, Ada senior had herself been in service before her marriage, and so would almost certainly have taught Ada junior whatever she could of her own superior professional skills to help prepare her daughter for likely tasks in the kitchen of an employer. Ada's paternal grandmother, Jane Parsons had also discovered the usefulness of culinary expertise in earning a living when early widowhood had made her the sole breadwinner. Back in the 1860s, she had enabled her children to survive and go to school by selling confectionery she made.

In the centre of the notebook, Ada tried to classify a long list of the dishes she named in her recipes. She also made notes on soups and other dishes to act as an aide memoire when preparing suitable lunch or dinner menus for different functions. It must have been challenging for someone who did not speak or understand French in their daily life to remember what many of these strange sounding delicacies were.

Initially, Ada had some difficulty spelling unfamiliar French cookery terms and names of dishes or ingredients. As time went by, however, she became more familiar with them and her confidence naturally grew, so the mistakes disappear.

The items Ada chose to record were recipes for dishes that were uncalled for in her day to day life. They were for special food to titillate the discriminating palates of wealthy employers and their guests. They included quantities and step by step methods. She did not feel the need to record such basic information as to how to make pastries of different types, how to cook and press a cow's tongue, how to make aspic, glazes or a good meat stock, nor how to clarify lard or butter or make a basic sauce. These things were everyday practices that she knew so well she could perform them automatically.

We have not included every single recipe of Ada in this book. All the unusual ones are here but not those that can be found in every basic cookery book, such as dinner rolls, omelette or brandy snaps. This recipe book is the only one belonging to Ada that has survived, but there could have been others that did not escape damage over the decades. This possibility is supported by the fact that there are numerous dishes on the menus of 1910-11 for which there are no recipes recorded in the book. For example "Saumon Sauce Genoise", "Cotelettes Poycestre", " Cailles a la Lucullus" and numerous others (*see menus*).

Therefore it must be seen as an incomplete picture of the type of food prepared in the kitchens of the various gentry for whom Ada worked.

In preparing the recipes for publication, so that any readers who wish to might try them out, we have added in some of the steps Ada did not bother to write because she would have understood what to do. We have also given oven temperatures in approximate degrees Celsius instead of the rather vague descriptive terms such as "moderate oven", "hot oven" or " a quick fire".

A few of the ingredients in the recipes are not familiar to the modern kitchen. While some still are available in the same form as in 1910, such as gelatine sheets, or anchovy paste, others may have to be substituted with modern alternatives. For example "King of Oudes Sauce", for which probably any hot pepper sauce would work, was a commercially available exotic bottled sauce of the colonial era. "Harvey's" would presumably mean some quality sherry still available by that name."Carmine" refers to cochineal red food colouring. One recipe calls for a preparation named "crème de riz" which is rice flour, mixed with water or milk (*50g flour, 75g liquid*) and steamed before use in the recipe. Croutons feature in many of the hors d'oevres, but they must have been dainty slices of baguette toasted and not the little cubes we understand by that name today. Otherwise the foodstuffs required are probably easier to find today than they were then.

Some of the terms refer to equipment used then which is not appropriate in a modern kitchen. For example many dishes had to be "salamandered" with the use of a special hot iron passed over it before serving. Today we see the use of kitchen blow torches by chefs to accomplish the same result. Although we have left in the instructions to pass mixtures "through a wire sieve" as Ada had to, it would be much more convenient and quicker to put the mixture through a blender nowadays. However, the wire sieve is still the Michelin preferred method for ensuring there are no pips in a fruit puree.

The type of functions Ada had to cater for are suggested by her menus dated 1910 and 1911 and also in the names of the recipes. Shooting parties were a popular pursuit and so the frequent inclusion of game such as pheasant, hare, rabbit, pigeon or even larks is no surprise. Perhaps "Shooting cake" was a useful snack for the participants to take into the field as a picnic if not to be part of the lunch table on their return.

While many dishes could be part of an everyday breakfast, luncheon, afternoon tea or dinner served to a small family group, some were clearly intended to be for showy entertainment."Pouding electric light" must have been intended as a spectacular talking point at a society evening dinner party. The canapés and entrees are the usual fare of large receptions or cocktail parties and conjure up a vision of the glittering society function that must have been a frequent occurrence chez the Marquis and Marchioness of Winchester at Amport house. The Dalgetys too at Lockerley, would have entertained business associates

and socialites in a similar manner. None of the quantities given in the recipe book are for a large scale affair, but a cook of Ada's experience could easily multiply for increased quantities according to the numbers being catered for.

A cook of Ada's background and experience would have been involved in the day to day meal preparation for the family as well as for the servants below stairs. She would also cook at important banquets and functions but the prestigious occasions would doubtless have involved bringing in a high class chef schooled in Haute Cuisine perhaps in Paris or a top London hotel and the rest of the kitchen staff would assist in preparation under his direction.

One of the menus contains a dish for turtle: "Tortue a la Keine" which was a delicacy afforded only by the super rich who would have been familiar with Turtle soup. At the kitchen of Burghley House in Lincolnshire, is a special turtle-shaped copper tureen for serving the soup and a set of fourteen turtle skulls, which illustrate that even at Burghley, it was seldom served but was a spectacular treat for rare occasions. Dishes using foiegras, truffles, caviar, oysters, quail and lobster, are numerous, however. Offal, especially calf sweetbreads also feature quite a lot. These and dishes flavoured with anchovies, olives, camembert or parmesan must have been far more expensive and exotic than they are to us today. Only the wealthy could afford such luxuries when the majority of the English population could barely afford to put meat on the table once a week. The frequency with which these ingredients were incorporated into the menus in Ada's book serves to show that her employers not only had expensive taste and the wealth to support it, but also that they were making an ostentatious display for the approval of their social equals.

Mediterranean ingredients like olives, anchovies and artichokes not known to most English inhabitants until the 1960s, were part of the everyday diet of the rich at the start of the twentieth century. They were the only ones who could think of travelling to France, Italy, Switzerland or Germany in the pre war years. People like the Dalgetys and the Paulets had travelled widely outside Europe as well, so the use of Indian style spicy flavourings such as cayenne, and ginger were popular with them too. Asparagus was also a luxury vegetable that did not form part of the working man's diet unless, like Ada, they had tasted it in the course of preparing it and acquired a taste for it and a desire to emulate the habits of those they saw as their superiors.

Interestingly enough none of the recipes contain garlic. It was socially unacceptable to the English at this time much more so than now. It was unladylike to breathe the smell of garlic into the face of your suitor. Given that many of the entertainment foods were aphrodisiacs, garlic would have been especially inappropriate to the licentious liaisons that often occurred at such soirees.

The usual first course on the menu seems to have been a light soup or consommé of which there were numerous variations. Fish courses of cold trout or salmon with a sauce or in aspic, whitebait, smelts, sole or turbot were included in dinner and banquet menus but omitted for lunches. In the main courses, Chaud froid (*cold jellied chicken coated in glaze or aspic or game with mayonnaise*) was a very fashionable dish to serve especially in the summer at this time and many of the desserts were steamed puddings. These were made special by the addition of exotic flavourings or fruit. Fancy jellies in different colours, soufflés, gateaux and mousses also featured. Ices were a novelty dish given that at this time only the very wealthy had an electricity supply or a refridgerator with freezer compartment. Vegetables did not form a large part of the fare on a menu and were not mixed with the other food in any of the dishes apart from soups and the unusual recipe of Lady Cavendish for "Cabbage Pudding". Peas were simply cooked in a tiny amount of water with a little butter and some sugar and mint, asparagus was steamed and served with melted butter, and sometimes "salade" was prepared and served as an accompaniment or separate course in the French style. Occasionally, tomatoes or mushrooms are mentioned in a recipe. Artichoke hearts were stuffed to be served as an hors d'oevre. By the addition of a cheese sauce in "Chouxfleur Gratin" cauliflower became more appealing to the diner, but there is no mention of any sauces on any other vegetables. Pesumably vinaigrette or mayonnaise was made available with the salad course. Sauces for the most part seem to have been made to enhance the steamed fish and stewed or roasted meat dishes. Potatoes are not mentioned anywhere. Could this be because they were the staple food of the poor? Bread was served in between courses with soup and with the meat course according to traditional French style. Otherwise bread found its way into the dessert as a constituent of the steamed pudding.

In some ways this kind of diet appears less healthy than current nutritionists recommend. This is because of the liberal use of butter and cream and eggs in the recipes. and the emphasis on meat and game. It was certainly a high protein diet with a lack of fibre and vitamins. Vegetables were steamed but bicarbonate of soda was added to improve the colour and this served to destroy the vitamin C. Fruit was stewed or candied and so again vitamins lost in the process. However, poultry and game and the fish served up were low in fat and free from the additives and preservatives used today since they were caught and used fresh. The ham would have been smoked and salted on the bone at a local butcher, whereas the tongue would have been skinned cooked and pressed by the cooks in the kitchen. The cooks themselves would also have skinned and boned the hares and rabbits, plucked, drawn and singed the feathers of the pheasants and other game birds and poultry, scaled and filleted the fish if they were not to be steamed whole and served on the bone.

Food preparation was far more laborious than today owing to the absence of electricity and the fact that small domestic processors had not yet been invented. Ada and her kitchen colleagues would therefore have spent a lot of time beating and whisking preparations for sauces, cakes and biscuits. If any puree needed making, the tedious job of pushing it through a wire sieve and collecting it in a bowl was the only way to do what now would take a couple of minutes in a blender. Bones and carcases would be boiled every day, the cooks then reduced, strained and clarified the stocks made from them and separated the gelatine from the fats, but wasted nothing as they would have been used to cook or flavour other foods.

Although later in life Ada would still never have been able to afford luxuries like truffles, oysters or lobster, she certainly put into practice many of the cookery techniques in her home life that she had learned in service and served up delicacies that other village families would never have tasted. She cooked and served pheasants, pigeons, rabbits and fish like salmon, trout and eels to her family. Often she served game or chicken cold and jellied in aspic and always included asparagus when it was in season. She followed her professional cooking practices at home and passed them down through the generations. Ada never used margarine, always butter or lard in pastries for the flavour, preferring to make rough puff instead of shortcrust. She always fried her meat in butter and deglazed the pan to make gravy from the meat juices and not from a packet Frequently, she would make good stock from bones and carcasses to turn it into consommé for soups or add it to a casserole.

It might seem strange to a reader born after 1960 to learn that royalty would have wanted to eat rabbits on a weekly basis when it seems such a lowly food nowadays (although currently regaining popularity in trendy restaurants). However the rabbits were almost certainly required for making rabbit stew for the servants' meals, especially during the First World War in 1914-18 when any meat was in short supply. Hare, and baby rabbit on the other hand, feature in the family menus just as pheasant, quail, partridges and pigeons. It is easy to overlook the fact that before commercial factory farm production made these creatures readily available for supermarkets, they were expensive items to obtain. This was because in order to catch them, you had to employ full time gamekeepers whose duty was to set snares and keep poachers away from them. Sometimes an estate had a warrener to do this job while the head gamekeeper concentrated on rearing pheasants and releasing them in the woods to fatten them and prepare them for the shooting season. This and putting captured poachers through court was a costly business. In addition, the aristocracy and gentry would often also have a river and fish keeper to monitor the stocks of salmon and trout and police the estate waters against night fish poachers. Poachers would take risks stealing any game from an estate to feed their own family or to sell on the black market so even for them it was an occasional treat normally reserved only for the rich. Servants eating rabbit stew were themselves a privileged group among their contemporaries. The difficulty and expense of hunting wild meat made it scarce and as such a luxury for any table. Game shooting was also the sport reserved for the privileged classes. Its presence on the menu indicated all the trappings of high society wealth and landed privilege. If it made a rare appearance on the table of a peasant household, it was usually illicit and relished as a forbidden fruit.

# Ada Emma Parsons

*Ada aged 21*

B orn in Swallowsfield West, Wokingham, Berkshire on 3rd August 1888, Ada was the eldest of seven children. She had a humble beginning but yet a privileged one for a country peasant girl. Her father, William George Parsons, was a domestic groom from Gloucestershire. He had a relatively well paid and interesting job which took him out of his home world into the world of the wealthy and famous[1]. Working with the personal horses and carriages and the conveyance of dignitaries to their business and social engagements was a position of skill, experience and above all, trust. It required discretion, and responsibility for the employer's safety and security. Before marrying him, Ada's mother, Ada Emma Saunders, together with the latter's elder sister Emma, had both been domestic servants to an elderly widow named Ann Walker, living at 11 Sheffield Terrace in Kensington, Chelsea, whose profession was in *"Dividends"* according to the 1881 census. Experiencing life in town as

[1] Born in Bibury, Gloucestershire in 1856 to a father who had been servant to the miller of Midford, Oxon and a mother who on being widowed by the time William was 5, became a confectioner to feed and clothe her four young children. There was a huge gulf between William's background and that of his employer in 1891.

well as country and seeing from close quarters the lifestyle of the middle classes and gentry, must have been an incentive to these country folk at a time of exciting political and social changes.

*William Parsons at his place of work*

By the time Ada was 2 years old, in 1891, she had a 7 month old brother named William George and the family were now living at 34 Reading road, Stratfield Turgiss, Hampshire. Her father William had been unusually fortunate in attending a primary school in his home village, Bibury, at the age of five a decade before schooling was compulsory in the country and especially since his widowed mother was struggling to feed her four children all at school, by making and selling sweets. Following the introduction of compulsory education in 1870, her mother Ada had also been among the first of her social class to attend primary school in her home town of Asthall, Oxfordshire, (*she is recorded at age 8 as being a "scholar" in the 1871 census*). Ada junior must also have attended primary school, if not in Stratfield Turgiss, then definitely at Fleet, Hartley Witney, Hampshire where her family were all living by 1901.

Her primary school grounding imbued a strict sense of morals that underpinned her life. She remained a faithful member of the High Church congregation. Her neat and careful handwriting and good spelling recorded in her notebook were the result of the free primary education given in her local school.

---

*Ada and her brother
William taken about 1895*

Her education was furthered at the age of 14, in 1901, when she began work as a servant in the household of George B Northcote, Conservative agent, in the Manor House at Cove St John, Hartley Witney. There, the Northcote family consisted of George's Irish born wife, Charlotte and their three children: Gwendoline (*aged* 16), Sybil (*aged* 11) and Spencer (*aged* 11). Four domestic servants worked for the family: Ada, a single mother aged 48 named Annie Mays and her two sons William (*aged* 19) and Edgar (*aged* 15). It seems reasonable to assume that the two boys would have done the heavy work, leaving Ada to be under the direction of Annie in the kitchen and parlour and as a chamber maid.

As a domestic, Ada was living in at the Manor, yet would occasionally have had the opportunity to see her family living nearby at Hartley Witney. William George, her now 40 year old father, may even have been the domestic Coachman for the Northcote family. If not, he worked for another dignitary in the area.

At home Ada's mother was busy rearing her other children, who by now numbered five. William, who was now 13 and probably also working, Frederick (11), Horace (9), Lily (4) and Ernest (2). With so many young mouths to feed, Ada junior would have to earn her own keep and live away from home as there would have been little space in Vine Cottage with the rest of her family.

*Photo above: William George Parsons in his uniform.*

*Ada's mother, Brother Jackie and Father William George at Vine cottage, Church Road, Fleet.*

However, she was to keep in contact with them as she travelled far and wide across the country in the next decade or two as the scribblings in her notebooks and on the back of her photo collection reveal.

At some time between 1901 and 1915, Ada had the opportunity to go to Scotland. She was living at Glenmazeran Lodge, Tomatin in Invernesshire. One of her siblings sent her a postcard addressed to her while she was there in 1910. She was presumably working for the owner who in 1911 was Captain F.J.Dalgety (*see, page xvii* ).

By 1909 she was working at the Marquess of Winchester's House: Amport House, at Amport St Mary, Andover, Hampshire, together with Mrs Alice Hughes (*see photo opposite*).

*Alice Hughes        Ada Parsons*
*Ada was in her 21st year and quite the Edwardian Lady on her day off.*

It must have been here that she gained her grounding in the art of cookery and such French language as she needed to know in catering for the rich and famous of the day. At the time she was there, the 16th Marquess was Henry William Montague Paulet (*1862-1962*) who, having been educated at the Royal Navy Academy, Gosport, shunned a life at sea and instead went big game hunting in the Rocky Mountains, toured India, China, Ceylon and Japan and in the 1890s went out on a lion hunting expedition with Cecil Rhodes. The Marquess served as Lord Lieutenant of Hampshire and Chairman of Hampshire County Council 1904-1909, so would have been at home during the time Ada worked at Amport. The food that she had to cook

*Ada Parsons far right*

in the menus of 1909 to 1911 in her notebook reflect the tastes of her widely travelled employer and his family and guests. Some of the recipe names even suggest this.

On one of the central pages of her recipe book, where she has listed numerous haute cuisine dishes and made brief explanatory notes about them,

*Ada Parsons        Alice Hughes*
*Ada at work in Amport House Kitchen with Alice Hughes*

*Glemazeran Lodge Tomatin circa 1957*
*Photograph by David White kind permission of Am Baile Highland Photographic Archive*

she has written her name and address as *"Ada Parsons, Lockerley Hall, Romney, Hants"*.   According to the 1911 census she was here in 1911 as a kitchen maid under the cook Margery Wise.   Frederick Gonnerman Dalgety, a business tycoon who had made a fortune in the American goldrush the flour business and the Australian wool trade, had built Lockerley Hall[2] in 1867-8, and Frederick J. Dalgety, his son and heir, was the owner of the hall in 1911.   Perhaps some of the extravagant dishes in the book were to entertain the Dalgetys and their guests.

*Picture of the Bowes Lyon family with Lady Elizabeth front row left, also Countess*
*Strathmore, and Lady Elphinstone, Back row, left to right Lord Elphinstone, Lord Glamis.*
*Lord Strathmore, Colonel Malcolm Bowes-Lyon, James Stuart.*

At some time between then and 1915, Ada must have moved to the employ of the Bowes Lyon family at the Bury St Paul's Walden Hertfordshire and this is probably where she met and fell in love with the man she was to marry.   He was Francis Charles Mattin, Head Gamekeeper to the Earl of Strathmore on his estate at St Paul's Walden, Hertfordshire.   Their wedding took place on March 21st 1915 when she was 26 years old, and Francis two years her senior, at St John's Church, Clapham rise, Wandsworth District, Greater London.   Ada was at that time living at 44 Gaskell Street, Wandsworth. The Earl of Strathmore was, in January 1915, at 20 St James Square London, from where he wrote to Francis about a shoot at the end of January, but was to be at Glamis Castle in the middle of the month and also later in the year since he sent letters to Francis from Glamis in October and December of that year. It is not clear whether Ada was in London working for The Earl of Strathmore before her marriage or if she was working for someone else at Gaskell Street[3].

Francis had lived all his life in Hertfordshire and Bedfordshire and since the age of 4, his father had been the head gamekeeper to the Earl of Strathmore. It is more than a coincidence, however that Francis's father, William, had lived all his formative years in Hampshire in Elvetham, the next village to Hartley Whitney where the Parsons family lived. It seems that the two families must have known each other or known of each other long before the marriage took place. Frank was not living at home in East Hall with the rest of the family when the 1901 census was taken, so it is possible that he was staying with his grandfather, Charles Mattin, the head gamekeeper at Elvetham manor, Hartney Whitney in Hampshire at that time. Maybe as a 14 year old, he was gaining work experience with his grandfather. This could have enabled him to strike up a relationship with Ada. Wherever he was, by the time the next census came round in 1911, Frank was a 24 year old gamekeeper working alongside his father at St Paul's Walden.

*William Mattin head gamekeeper and Laura his wife when working on the Strathmore estate at The Bury, St Paul's Walden.*

It remains a matter for conjecture as to whether Ada got her job at the Bury because of Frank's father already working there, or whether it was as a result of connections between her former employers, the Marquess and Marchioness of Winchester and the

---

[3] Since the Strathmore Estate records do not name servants individually, but refer to them in groups such as "housemaids" or "gamekeepers", it is not possible to trace an exact record of employment, which forces us to rely on oral evidence from family members alive at the time corroborated by letters and census evidence.

Bowes Lyon Family[4].   It is also possible that she got the job through an agency in London, since these were operating at the time and the usual method of obtaining service jobs with the gentry and aristocracy.   At any rate, since Frank's father, William, died in 1913 aged only 49, his eldest son Frank[5] took over as head gamekeeper at the estate.   The Earl of Strathmore subsequently sent Frank's mother, the widowed Laura, who till then had been living in

*Patrick Bowes Lyon*

the lodge with all three of William's children, up to Scotland where he sponsored the education of Frank's two siblings Dora and Hubert[6].   Frank was now living at East Hall alone.   As World War I broke out, Frank was not able to do military service owing to his paralysed arm.   The Earl's son and heir, Patrick Bowes Lyon, served with the Black Watch regiment, of which his father was Honorary Colonel. A photograph of his son in uniform was given to Frank who was about the same age as him.   Patrick's brother, Captain Fergus, also served with the Black watch, in the 8th battalion.   He was killed on the battlefield while leading an attack on German lines in the Battle of Loos.   The Earl wrote to Frank on October 22nd 1915 about a wages account and added "*I now thank you so much for your kind reference to our dear son, who made the supreme sacrifice for his country and I am sure you feel <u>with</u> us and <u>for</u> us*" indicating that Frank knew Fergus personally.

Her Ladyship became very ill as a result of the loss of her son and that fact is also referred to by the Earl in some of his letters to Frank between 1916 and 1922.

---

[4] Or the Bowes Lyons and the Dalgetys, since by 1930, Glenmazeran Lodge had been purchased by Lord and Lady Elphinstone, a sibling of the Earl of Strathmore, which suggests a social connection between them and the Dalgetys.
[5] Inspite of his disability caused by childhood Polio.
[6] Dora was trained to be a music teacher in Scotland and Hubert went to university in Scotland training in metallurgy.

Michael Claude Hamilton Bowes Lyon, a younger son, was taken prisoner of war during World War I but lived on after the war.   Frank also knew him personally, as he recorded in his shooting year book on May 14th and on June 8th 1930 "Captain Michael came to the rearing field in afternoon".

Ada was, after their marriage, able to move into the gamekeeper's Lodge with him. She presumably still worked in the household until her first pregnancy and also in between children when they were at school.

*The gamekeepers' lodge at East Hall in the 1920s*

By 23rd April 1916, World War I was in full swing when her first child, Lorna Ada Mattin was born.   Ada was designated *"gamekeeper's wife"* on the birth certificate.   The war came closer to home than any might have expected as the German zeppelins by now had started to fly over Britain on bombing raids. Frank must have written to Earl Claude about one flying over within sight of the Bury as in a reply to Frank dated October 4th 1916 from Glamis Castle, the Earl wrote, " *it must have been most wonderfully interesting to see the Zepp so long overhead, and to have been there to see it catch* *fire and fall.   I am truly glad they bagged it. "*Clearly this refers to the shooting down of the Zeppelin by Britain's first anti-aircraft guns. He goes on," *I must thank you for your letter about the fire.   There is much damage done but the fire damage can be repaired, as the stone stood well, but the water damage was serious to pictures, ceilings and other things*".   Presumably this fire refers to one at Glamis but whether its cause was an incendiary attack or just a domestic accident is not stated.   As she was now a mother, Ada's catering henceforth was concentrated on her immediate family, and her energies to bringing up three young children of her own as John was born in 1920 and another daughter, Zena, born in 1925, all at East Hall.

During the 1910s and early 1920s Elizabeth Bowes Lyon, Her Majesty the late Queen Mother, was still living sometimes at the Bury with her father and sometimes at his London address, 20 St James Square.   In November 1918 she wrote a letter to Frank on behalf of *"her Ladyship"*, requesting him *"to send up a few more rabbits weekly,  as there are more people in the house just now"*

*Letter from Elizabeth Bowes Lyon
to Francis Mattin*

The Lady Elizabeth referred to her father's cook affectionately as *"Mattie"*, making her feel something of a favourite and especially liked her bread and butter pudding.

Albert and Elizabeth, were married on 26th April 1923 and Francis and Ada received an invitation to view the royal wedding presents at Buckingham Palace.   They also received a piece of the royal wedding cake which is still kept as a family heirloom.   After  their marriage, Elizabeth and Albert, (*later to become George VI*) were frequent visitors along with their two daughters Elizabeth and Margaret.

The princess Elizabeth was a year younger than Zena, Ada's youngest. Clara Knight the nanny of the two princesses would often visit her brother Harry's farm on the estate, which was situated close to Keepers Cottage. There the children would often play together in the farm yard. Zena would recollect how Princess Elizabeth would take charge of the games and once she had the idea of playing a Naval game with boats made of leaves and twigs. They built a harbour from stones and mud and to fill this with water, they scribed a channel from the farm yard pond where the cattle would drink, leading a rivulet of water down to fill their harbour and float the boats. Time came for tea and the children were called off to their respective meals. Later Zena was alerted by a commotion outside. Her father Frank and Harry Knight were out in the lane knee deep in water. While they had been eating their tea the small channel that filled their harbour had been eroded by the water and the entire contents of the pond emptied into the yard and lane. Zena confessed and being the eldest was sent to bed in punishment. However, she was fortunate enough to be given a book by the princess, which must have made up for taking the blame. The volume *"The FABLES of ÆSOP"* with beautiful full page colour plate illustrations by Edward J.Detmold was to become her most prized possession.

During his time as Head gamekeeper, it was Frank's job to arrange shoots for the Earl of Strathmore and his guests. One visitor was a very special one, namely the Duke of York, before he became His Royal Highness, King George VI. He wrote a letter of thanks to Frank for the shoot during the Christmas of 1928 along with a photograph of himself, *"for the New Year"*. *(Both of these items are now treasured family heirlooms)*.

*The Duke of York and the Earl of Strathmore, Christmas Shoot 1928*

*Inset:Duke of York's Letter to Frank Mattin*                         *Photo of the Duke of York, presented to Frank Mattin*

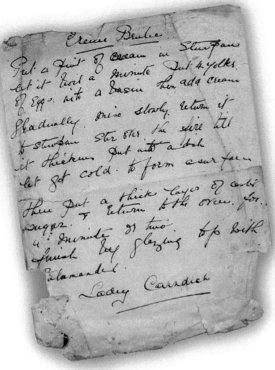

*Lady Cavendish's Creme Brulee*

Ada had kept a number of loose leaf recipes in her book signed *"Lady Cavendish"* or marked *"Lady Cavendish's receipt"* which must refer to *"her ladyship"*, Cecilia Cavendish-Bentink, the Countess of Strathmore who was the Earl Claude's wife. One of these recipes is for cabbage pudding and another is for *"Poulet Diable Blanc"*. These support the oral evidence we have that Ada cooked for the Earl and Countess as well as for the Lady Elizabeth and her friends.

Contrary to many accounts which describe the life *"below stairs"* at this time as being low paid drudgery reluctantly undertaken because it was one of the few types of available work, in Ada's and Frank's case, it was viewed quite differently. It was an opportunity to acquire a skilled profession and a rewarding and creative occupation superior to others open to them. It was a privilege for them to come into contact with the family and associates of their employers, to be respected by them and trusted with the important responsibilities they were given. They were generously remunerated, as the example below shows, and allowed to take holidays on request. A letter to Frank from the Earl at Glamis on 30th March 1920 tells him: *"Certainly take your leave as soon as ever you like. I suppose you will make arrangements for the ground to be looked after when you are away"*. None of this portrays a picture of downtrodden servants struggling on the breadline and denied personal freedoms. Admittedly, discipline within the household would have been strict, but such discipline was self imposed by individuals who saw the need for living an orderly life, showed personal respect for their employers and had a sense of pride in their work. Frank and Ada were two such individuals and they reaped the benefits. The family remained at East Hall and the children started school in the next village at Whitwell. Lorna, despite the fact that she had passed the examination to attend the local grammar school, was not allowed to go because she had to take over her mother's role in parenting her siblings while her mother worked.

*Frank, Ada, Lorna and John in the family Morgan*

Thanks to the generous remuneration for his work by the Earl, (in a 1922 letter, along with five percent of the £235 value of game Frank sold for him from the season's shoots, he sent Frank a Christmas present of 5 guineas), Frank had now become affluent enough to own a motor car shown here some time in the 1920s. He and his family were well fed and well dressed and had comfortable accommodation by the standards of the day. Although we have no record of Ada's own wages, she certainly benefitted from those of her husband.

*Mr Jackson photographed in 1924
when seventy years old*

A local wealthy gentleman farmer and cattle breeder named William Jackson and his wife had been close associates of the Mattin and Lucas (*Frank's mother's*) family for many years. According to William Mattin's shooting register dated 1894-1899, William Jackson had often attended shoots or purchased game from the shoots on the estate. Mr Jackson's name appears several times in the register alongside Reverend Clowes and other members of the Clowes family who at other times accompanied Lord Glamis on shoots or ferreting at Hitchwood or Almshoebury on the Strathmore Estate. Some time before 1918, the Jacksons retired and moved to the stylish bungalow they had had built in Grange road, Blunham, Bedfordshire.

Throughout his life, Mr Jackson had kept a daily diary of his activities and both he and his wife were orderly record-keepers. His diaries survive, along with her address book and together they provide evidence that Frank was a frequent visitor to Blunham in the years immediately after World War I, sending loins of venison or rabbits and pigeons to Mr Jackson at regular intervals and receiving pieces of dress material for his little girl or taking away eggs. Mr Jackson and his wife had frequently travelled by train from Blunham to London to the theatre and to buy boots or clothes and so clearly he was wealthy. He had, before retirement, won numerous trophies for his prize cattle at agricultural shows in the latter part of the 19th century.

Being about the same age as William Mattin, Mr Jackson had been William's close friend and shooting partner and clearly regarded Frank as the son he did not have. Frank no doubt looked on Mr Jackson as the father figure he no longer had after 1913 and felt a duty of care. By the time Lorna was 16, in 1932, Mr Jackson had an ailing wife and needed a live-in nurse and housemaid. Frank therefore did not hesitate in sending along his wife, Ada, to perform this service, so she left the family at East Hall to be looked after by Lorna, and moved in at The Bungalow, Blunham. We must, for lack of evidence, speculate that she resigned from her duties at the Bury in order to do this[7].

---

During the late 1930s, Lorna and the rest of the family now moved to Blunham to be nearer to their mother while she cared for Mr Jackson, his wife now dead. They first lived in rented rooms at *"The Horseshoes"* public house. They soon rented a home called *"Prospect House"* on Blunham Hill.

Mr Jackson passed away in 1940 and once probate had passed, Grange Farm and all its chattels and livestock became the possession of Frank Mattin. It seemed an appropriate time to become self employed. Frank resigned from his post as head

[7] The Estate records of how Lord Strathmore and his Elder son managed St Paul's Walden Bury or who was employed, were not left behind for their successors so although it is thought there that Frank Mattin was succeeded by Bert King in 1931 or 1932, there must have been a period of overlap as Frank definitely left in the mid to late thirties.

gamekeeper at a time when the elderly Earl Claude Bowes Lyon was becoming increasingly frail and was soon to be succeeded by his eldest son Patrick in 1944. Frank retained his connection with game keeping, renting a wood near Gransden in Cambridgeshire, and organising shoots. He did this in his spare time whilst he maintained and ran the small farm. The family all moved into the farm house their father now owned. They had suddenly become members of the middle class with their own home and a poultry and duck farm to sustain them.

Frank became one of the few residents of Blunham to own a car during a time when the Great Depression was causing so much hardship to many others.

(*See letter opposite*)

T. A. OVERFIELD, Engineer.

SERVICE DEPOT FOR

THE INTERNATIONAL HARVESTER COMPANY OF GREAT BRITAIN, LIMITED.

80 DRIFFIELD. **DRIFFIELD**. E. YORKS.

AUTHORISED MAIN DISTRICT DEALER FOR
INTERNATIONAL MOTOR TRUCKS, TRACTORS AND OIL ENGINES.

March 16 th. 1938.

Dear Mr. Jackson,

Thank you ever so much for your parcel and for your letter of the 8 th. of March.

I am sorry I am late in answering and thanking you for same, but, I am so busy just now TRYING to get money in from Farmers, I have used every method there is -, I THINK, when you come over to Driffield again you will have to go round with me to see IF IT HAS ANY EFFECT.

Anyhow, we are all keeping well I think at this end and Myself still busy with The Aerodrome and by the look of things I am likely to be for some time.

I dare say in your district the same as here people are begining to realise the seriousness of the UNREST of Mr Hitler, all we can do is GET READY FOR THE HOUND in my opinion. If you saw the Aerodrome now you would be very impressed, in fact, I get lost myself when visiting round.

I have got a new ESTATE CAR and I should like you to have a ride in it. -: some people say it is like an East-Yorkshire Bus, some say it is like A Hearse, but anyhow, it suits me and I am sure it will suit YOU WHEN you get into it.

Drop me a line when you are coming to Driffield again and IF AT ALL POSSIBLE I WILL MEET YOU AT THE STATION IN REAL STYLE.

I hope you are keeping in good health, both Mrs. Overfield and Myself wish to thank you very much indeed for your very kind rememberances.

Yours very truly.

Mr Jackson's will made Frank a residuary legatee of the estate, which included nearly £3,000 worth of stock and dividends on the London and North Eastern Railway and the London, Midland and Scottish Railway. After duties and expenses, Frank received the sum of £1,300 which was a considerable windfall in December 1940.

The letter received by Mr Jackson in 1938, two years before he died, reveals the state of farmers' finances during the inter war period of economic depression and also the feelings towards Hitler and the impending war. Clearly the affluent, such as Mr Jackson's business correspondent, did not have to forego the pleasure of a new vehicle even while his customers were struggling to pay their debts. Although well provided for by their benefactor's bequest, Frank,

*Ada, Frank, Lorna, Zena and Ada's dog, posing for photo to send John in North Africa.*

Ada and their children all worked hard on the farm during the war years from 1939-45, since every scrap of food that could be home produced was needed by the besieged population. Francis did not serve in the military in this war nor the first one, because he had a paralysed and withered arm as a result of polio in infancy. Their son, John, however, served with the R.A.F. in North Africa. The two girls, Lorna and Zena both helped with the rearing of poultry and vegetable and fruit production for the market. Zena was denied permission to join the WAAF because her father, Frank, needed her

*John Mattin 1939*

as a farm labourer. While no evacuee children were assigned to the Mattin farm, neighbours had to take them in and many problems were caused to villagers who did. Two boys from London staying in Grange road, stole all the savings of their aged host because he stored it in his wardrobe.

One of the most unpleasant jobs Ada had to do during the war in the day to day farm work was to cut up the "Tottenham Pudding" which farmers had to buy as stock feed for pigs and chickens. This product was London Council kitchen waste that had been boiled up, pressed and packaged for farmers to buy. By all accounts it was nasty stuff, smelled like sewage and the family were suspicious that it was likely to be a disease carrier to its handlers. It was a far cry from preparing Beignets for Caviar or Filets de Lievres aux Cerises for the Paulets or the Bowes Lyons, but the War had changed all that for ever. A different society emerged at the end of it, more upwardly mobile and revolutionary than the Mattins could ever have imagined.

*Ada, dressed for church, about 1956*

In 1958, after a long painful battle with stomach cancer, aged 70 years, Ada passed away at her home, The Bungalow.

# The Recipes

## Ada Parsons

# LIST OF RECIPES

# HORS D'OEVRES

### AND

## CANAPES

# Bateau a l'Indienne

*Short crust pastry*

*Shrimps*

*Curry sauce*

## Method

1. Make short crust pastry tartlets in boat shaped moulds and bake them blind.

2. Make a good curry sauce and put the shrimps in it to heat through.

3. Put the mixture into the tartlets and serve.

# Beignets for Caviare

*10 oz flour*

*½ oz yeast*

*½ pt cream*

*½ pt warm water*

*A little salt*

*A little whipped white of an egg*

## Method

1. Dissolve the yeast in the warm water.

2. Sift the flour with the salt.

3. Mix in the warm water and other ingredients.

4. Set the sponge the same as for bread.

5. When well risen, fry in clarified butter like little pancakes.

6. Serve the beignets hot with caviar in jar handed round at same time.

# Canapes a la Marlborough.

Savoury biscuits
Foiegras
Hardboiled eggs
Parsley

**Method**

1. Cover biscuits with foiegras.

2. Garnish with yolks of hardboiled eggs and Parsley.

# Canapes a la Windsor

**Version 1:-**

Croutons
A little oil for frying
Foiegras
Tarragon
Butter
Cold cooked chicken
Cold pressed tongue

**Method**

1. Fry croutons in oil.

2. Spread foiegras on it.

3. Place small rounds of chicken and tongue.

4. Pipe tarragon butter round.

**Version 2**

Cold cooked chicken , ham and game
Parmesan cheese
3 anchovies  washed and boned
1 pat of butter
Cayenne
Croutons

**Method**

1. Pound ingredients together and pass through a wire sieve.

2. Have ready some fried bread croutons and spread mixture on  each.

3. Sprinkle with brown bread crumbs.

4. Place in the oven.

5. Serve very hot.

# Casselettes de Crevettes

Shrimps
Parmesan cheese
Puff pastry

## Method

1. Make pastry, roll out and cut out rounds to fit in little tartlet moulds.

2. Bake pastry cases blind in a moderate oven preheated at 180°c. for about 10 minutes.

3. Cook shrimps and fill the cases with them.

4. Cover the shrimps with grated parmesan cheese.

# Croutes a la St James

Small round croutons
Tomatoes
Mushrooms
Herrings roes

## Method

1. Have ready some fried bread croutons.

2. Place a slice of tomato on each and a slice of mushroom.

3. Place a herring roe on top of each, season and grill.

4. Serve hot.

# Croutes de Langue Froid

(cold tongue croutons )
Cold pressed tongue
Mayonnaise
Croutons (small rounds of French bread fried lightly)
Hard boiled eggs
Mustard cress

## Method

1. Make puree from the cold tongue and a little mayonnaise.

2. Pipe the tongue puree around the edge of the croutons.

3. Fill in the centre with chopped egg whites and a circle of sieved egg yolks in the centre of that.

4. Garnish each with a sprinkle of mustard cress.

# Croutes Epicurienne

Croutons of French Bread
Fresh salmon puree
Prawns (cooked and shelled)
Butter
Fresh herb such as dill or fennel

## Method

1. Have some fried croutons ready.

2. Finely chop the herbs and mix well with the softened butter.

3. Pass the cooked flaked salmon through a wire sieve and mix well with the herb butter, and prawns.

4. Spread the puree on the croutons.

# Croutes Francaise

Croutes shaped like small cutlets
Watercress
Butter
Caviar

## Method

1. Fry small cutlet-shaped croutes

2. Finely chop the watercress and mix it well with softened butter.

3. Pipe the watercress butter round the edge of the croutes.

4. Fill the centres with caviar.

# Croutes Rashel

Croutons
Slices of ham
Chicken livers
Small onion

## Method

1. Prepare croutons.

2. Cook chicken livers with a small chopped onion.

3. Push it through a wire sieve.

4. Season to taste.

5. Spread the chicken liver paste on the croutons.

6. Put on each crouton a slice of ham the same shape as a mushroom.

7. Serve hot.

# Foie a la Diable

Livers
Butter
Chutney
Curry powder
Glaze
Kings of Oudes sauce (hot pepper sauce)
Croutons

**Method**

1. Cut the livers up in small dice.

2. Saute very sharp (on a high heat?).

3. Then make the sauce with a little butter, chutney, Kings of Oudes sauce, little curry powder and a little glaze. Mix in the livers.

4. Make round croutons. Take the centres out.

5. Dish the livers in them.

# Gondolas de Camembert

Oblong cases of Puff Pastry
4 oz Cold cooked chicken (minced)
2-3 tablespoons Cream
Mustard
1 Camembert cheese
1 hardboiled egg
Breadcrumbs

**Method**

1. Bake blind the puff pastry cases.

2. Pass half the camembert cheese through a wire sieve and mix it with the minced chicken, the cream and mustard.

3. Season to taste and then put it into a forcing bag and pipe it into the prepared cases.

4. Cover half the top of each with sieved hardboiled egg yolk and the other half with rasped bread-crumbs.

5. Brown in the oven for a few minutes. Serve very hot.

# Hors d'Oevres Muscovite

Artichoke hearts
Chopped parsley
Lemon juice
Pepper
Oil
Caviar
Stoned olives stuffed with anchovy puree
Tabasco sauce

**Method**

1. Sprinkle artichoke hearts with lemon juice, chopped parsley pepper and oil.

2. Fill the centres with caviar and then an olive stuffed with anchovy paste.

3. Sprinkle with Tabasco sauce.

# Les Oeufs a la Diable

6 Eggs
1 oz Butter
2 tablespoons Cream
1 spoon curry powder
1 spoon French mustard
1 spoon chutney
½ spoon English mustard

**Method**

1. Fry 4 eggs in half of the butter.

2. Cut out with a cutter

3. Make mixture of ½ oz butter, the cream, curry powder and mustards and 2 raw yolks.

4. Stir this over the fire till it thickens.

5. Pour it over the fried eggs and salamander over.

6. Garnish with croutons and ham.

# Merluche

Dried haddock (substitute smoked haddock)
Butter
Toast
Eggs

**Method**

1. Poach the haddock in a little water.

2. Flake it off the bone.

3. Butter the toast and spread the flaked haddock on it.

4. Scramble the egg add a little butter and seasoning and spread it over the haddock.

# Mousse de Faisan a la York

1 pheasant that has been boiled in a good game stock

1 teaspoon of Bovril or glaze

Salt, pepper,

2 onions

¼ pint Espagnole sauce

1 ½ gill cream (whipped)

1 wine glass port

2 egg whites

1 oz (fresh) gelatine

truffles

chervil or tarragon

### Method

1. Rub the cooked pheasant through a fine sieve.

2. Add the glaze, salt, pepper , onions, gelatine and espagnole sauce.

3. Before it gets set, add the whipped cream and port.

4. Whip the egg whites till stiff, stir up together with the mousse (and then chill to set.)

5. Garnish with tarragon, chervil, truffles.

# Olives a la Mersaise

Anchovy pastry (short crust pastry, anchovy essence)

Olives (or olives stuffed with anchovy paste)

Anchovy butter

Mayonnaise

### Method

1. Make shortcrust pastry adding some anchovy essence to the mixture at the same time as adding water.

2. Roll out the pastry and fill greased boat -shaped moulds to make the required number of tartlets.

3. Prick the bases with a fork. Bake them blind for 7-10 minutes (at 170°c.).

4. If not using ready stuffed olives, stuff the olives with anchovy butter.

5. Mix the stuffed olives with mayonnaise and fill the boatlets with them.

# Oeufs a la Percy

*Eggs*
*Double cream*
*Cream Cheese*

**Method**

1. Hard boil the eggs.

2. Whip the cream and mix well with cream cheese.

3. Halve the eggs and place cut side down on serving platter,

4. Pipe the cream cheese mixture into a decorative rosette on each one.

5. Serve.

# Sandwiches a l'Adelaide

*Cold cooked chicken*
*Curry sauce*
*Croutons*

**Method**

1. Have ready some fried croutons

2. Prepare curry sauce

3. Finely chop the chicken, mix with the curry sauce and place some of the mixture between two fried croutons.

# Sandwiches a l'Indienne

*Anchovy fillets*
*Ham*
*Cooked chicken*
*Bread or savoury fingers*
*Curry sauce*

**Method**

1. Pound some anchovies with some cold ham and cold cooked chicken.

2. Mix in a good curry sauce .

3. Spread the savoury mixture between some savoury fingers or toast.

# Sardines a la Venetienne

*Thin slices of buttered bread with crusts removed*
*Sardines*

## Method

1. Spread the sardines on thinly sliced buttered bread

2. Roll up the slices and place on greased baking tray.

3. Bake them at 180°c to brown them.

# Savoury Pancakes

*Pancake batter*
*Savoury mince or caviar*

## Method

1. Prepare savoury mince by frying finely chopped onion with the minced chicken or beef.

2. Season it well.

3. Make very light thin pancakes.

4. Spread over some savoury mince and roll up.

5. Caviar can be used instead of mince.

# Souffles d' Homard Celestine

*Anchovy*
*1 teaspoon Anchovy essence*
*1 tablespoon thick cream*
*Carmine (cochineal)*
*Cayenne pepper*
*½ pint Aspic*
*2 tablespoons thick mayonnaise*
*Prepared lobster meat*

## Method

1. Pound anchovies in a mortar with anchovy essence, carmine, cayenne pepper and cream.

2. Pass through a sieve and mix in the aspic.

3. Whip together with mayonnaise whipped cream and finely chopped lobster meat.

4. Pour mixture into soufflé dishes and allow to set.

# Tartlets aux Macaroni

*Short crust pastry*
*Cut Macaroni pieces*
*Cheese*
*Cayenne pepper*
*Butter*

## Method

1. Make the short crust pastry and roll it out.

2. Cut rounds and line greased tartlet tins with them.

3. Prick bases lightly with a fork and bake blind for 10 minutes in an oven at 170°c.

4. Cook the cut macaroni and drain it well.

5. Fill the tartlets with it.

6. Work the butter, cheese and cayenne together well.

7. Put a spoonful of this mixture on top of the macaroni on each boat and brown with a salamander (under the grill).

# HOT ENTREES

# Cotelettes de Volaille a l'Ecarlate

Minced chicken

Mushroom essence

Cooked tongue

Cutlet shaped moulds

Lightly beaten egg yolk to glaze

## Method

1. Make some rather stiff forcemeat of chicken flavoured with mushroom essence.

2. Fill cutlet moulds with this mixture and poach them.

3. Cut the same number of cutlet shaped pieces of tongue.

4. Make hot and glaze the cutlets.

5. Arrange chicken and tongue cutlets alternately on serving plate. Serve demi-glazed.

# Croutes de Foie de Volaille

3 or 4 sets of chicken livers

1 tablespoon grated ham

1 tablespoon Chopped mushroom

1 tablespoon chopped onion

1 oz butter

Salt to taste

## Method

1. Chop the livers very fine.

2. Fry the chopped onion in the butter together with the livers.

3. Add the ham and mushroom

4. Season to taste.

5. Bind it all together with 1 teaspoon brown sauce.

6. Serve on croutes, very hot.

# Poulet a la Tartare

Fillets of roast chicken

½ pint batter

Oil for frying

Freshly made Tartare sauce

**Method**

1. Dip the fillets of chicken in the batter.

2. Fry in hot oil till golden brown.

3. Serve with Tartare sauce.

# Turbans de Volaille a la Gelee

Fillets of chicken

Foiegras

White chaud-froid   (mayonnaise)

**Method**

1. Cut rounds of chicken and cook them in the oven.

2. Put foiegras through a sieve and spread some between two rounds of chicken.

3. Arrange on serving dish and mask each with the white chaud-froid.

# Cotelettes de Perdreau a la Rachel

2 Partridges
Calves liver
Pork caul (pig's ears ,singed, cleaned and boiled in salted water)
A little butter for frying
Thyme
Parsley
Bay leaf
Salt and pepper
Mushrooms (pureed)
Brown sauce

**Method**

1. Bone the partridges.

2. Braise them and trim them into cutlet shapes.

3. Cut some calves liver into small pieces and fry together with parsley, thyme and bay leaf.

4. Pound and pass through a sieve, and if too dry add a little brown sauce and season.

5. Cover one piece of cutlet with liver and put in pieces of cooked pork caul (pig's ear).

6. Grill for 10 minutes.

7. Serve with puree of mushroom and glaze.


# Cotelettes de Pigeon Piedmontaise

Pigeons
Onion (chopped)
Parsley (chopped)
Ham (chopped)
Forcemeat (made with 1 lb minced chicken, pork or veal, seasoned and mixed with 2 egg whites)
2 Eggs
Breadcrumbs
Butter for frying

**Method**

1. Cut and bone the pigeons in two pieces.

2. Season with onion, parsley and ham.

3. Cook in stewpan. Press, then mask with forcemeat, egg and breadcrumbs.

4. Fry.

*Reeves Pheasant and other game courtesy of Antony Garrett Game Dealer*

# MAIN COURSES

# Chaud-froid de Poulet Printanier

Chicken

Aspic jelly

Cream

Egg white

Carmine colouring

Browning (from meat braising)

## Method

1. Braise the chicken and allow it to cool.

2. Cut it into portion sized pieces

3. Make the aspic jelly (by covering the carcass of the chicken and 3 lbs veal or beef knuckle bones, a carrot, an onion, a stick of celery and a bouquet garni with 4 pints of salted cold water, bring slowly to the boil and simmer for 2-4 hours to reduce it by half. Cool the stock and remove the fat. Clarify it by boiling with the white of an egg and skimming off the scum. When cool, pour the liquid through a napkin to strain it as clear as possible).

4. Allow to cool, but before it sets, mix three quarters of the aspic with the cream.

5. Colour one quarter with a little carmine (cochineal) to make a pink sauce.

6. Colour another quarter with the browning to make a brown sauce.

7. Mask (coat) an equal number of the cold chicken pieces in each of the three thick pink, white and brown chaud-froid sauces and allow to cool completely and set (in the refrigerator).

8. Arrange chopped clear aspic as a border around a serving dish and arrange the three colours of chaud-froid chicken attractively inside it.

# Chaudfroid de Mauvettes a l'Italienne

Larks (gutted with feathers removed)
Greaseproof paper
Butter
Cold cooked chicken
Cream
Aspic
Macedon viritalis (?)
Espagnole sauce

**Method**

1. Bone the larks.

2. Fill them with chicken cream

3. Wrap them in buttered paper.

4. Cook them in sauté pan.

5. Mask them over with a good espagnole sauce

6. Serve on aspic with macedon viritalis.


# Croustades A L'Indienne
## (Indian style croustades)

Plain forcemeat (made with minced chicken, cream and beaten egg)
Tongue slices
Curried mincemeat
Rice
Curried cream sauce (basic white sauce with a tablespoon of curry powder mixed into the roux)

**Method**

1. Butter small croustade moulds.

2. Garnish bottom with rounds of tongue

3. Line the moulds with plain forcemeat.

4. Fill them with curried mince.

5. Cover over with forcemeat and poach.

6. Dish up a border of cooked rice and in the centre, mix rice with curried mince.

7. Arrange the un-moulded poached croustades on the rice border.

8. Drizzle curried cream sauce over them.

# Epiprame

*Aspic jelly*
*Chicken forcemeat*
*Boiled  Tongue or ham*

## Method

1. Steam the chicken meat in a charlotte mould. Turn it out.

2. Cut in cutlettes. Also some boiled tongue or ham.

3. Pour some aspic jelly in the mould.

4. When set, arrange the cutlets 1 red 1 white.

5. Fill it with aspic. When set, turn out.

6. Fill centre with cut vegetables.

# Farce de Pigeon

*6 oz fresh pork or bacon*
*6 oz white meat*
*3 eggs*
*Pate de foie gras*
*4 good truffles*
*3 mushrooms*
*¼ pint tomato sauce*
*1 oz glaze*
*¾ pint aspic jelly*
*1 wineglass sherry*
*1 pinch sugar*

## Method

1. Pound the pork or bacon together with the white meat and pass through a sieve.

2. Season. Flatten the mixture on a wet slate and place in the centre 3 eggs, pate de foie gras cut in strips,

   4 good truffles cut up and 3 mushrooms.

3. Rollup and use (cook : presumably fry).

4. Boil up remaining ingredients all together and reduce to half the quantity.

   (Pour over the rolled cooked meat).

# Filets de Lievre aux Cerises
## (fillets of Hare with Cherries)

1 hare skinned and boned and prepared into fillets

Rice

Tomatoes

Cherries

**Method**

1. Lard and cook the fillets of hare.

2. Glaze them and dish them on a border of red rice.

3. Put a slice of tomato between each fillet.

4. Make a compote of cherries and place this in the centre.


# Filets de Sole a la Cardinale

Sole

Whiting (filleted)

1 lobster

Butter

**Method**

1. Fillet the Sole.

2. Make a forcemeat out of the whiting.

3. Take the spawn and the head from the lobster and pound them in the mortar with a little butter.

4. Then pass them through a sieve.

5. Mix them with the whiting and farcie the soles with the mixture and turn them over

   (i.e. roll them up).

6. Cook them in a sauté pan.

(presumably the lobster meat is prepared and sautéed to accompany the soles or be used in another dish).

# Medaillons a la Strasbourge

Cold cooked chicken
Aspic
Whipped cream
Truffles
Foiegras
Tongue
Horseradish cream

**Method**

1. Make a puree of the cooked chicken.

2. Mix it with the whipped cream.

3. Press the mixture into a shallow baking pan as a layer to cover the base and leave to set.

4. On top put a thin layer of truffles.

5. Cut a thin slice of tongue and foiegras and put on top.

6. Run a very thin white cream over and cut out with a round cutter.

7. Dish up on an aspic border and put in the centre horseradish cream.

# Pain a l'Indienne
## (Indian style Loaf)

Chicken (cooked and minced)
Slices of Ham
Truffles
Mushrooms
Curry sauce
Cream

**Method**

1. Make a cream of chicken (mixing minced chicken with the cream).

2. Mix in it some curry sauce.

3. Line a plain mould with the chicken mixture over the bottom and sides.

4. Place in the centre, minced chicken, truffles, mushrooms and ham, arranged attractively in layers with slices of ham last.

5. Allow to set . (Chill in refrigerator).

6. Turn out of the mould onto a serving dish.

7. Serve with curry sauce.

# Poulet Diable Blanc
## (Lady Cavendish's Receipt)

1 roasted chicken

¼ pint whipped cream

1 tablespoon Worcester sauce

1 tablespoon Harvey's

¼ tsp. Salt

Cayenne pepper

**Method**

1. Have a nice roasted chicken cut into pieces.

2. Make a white sauce with whipped cream, Worcester sauce, Harvey's and salt and

   a dash of cayenne pepper.

3. Place the chicken on a brown dish, pour the sauce over and brown in the oven.

4. Serve savoury rice separate.


# Ris de Veau a la Cheviot
## (Cheviot style calf sweetbreads)

Calf sweetbreads

Fillets of cooked pressed tongue

Prepared cooked Artichokes (globe)

**Method**

1. Braise small sweetbreads.

2. Dish them on a fillet of tongue.

3. Place each one in the bottom of an artichoke.

# Ris de Veau Belgravia

## (Calf Sweetbreads Belgravia)

Calf sweetbreads
Tongue
Truffles
Chestnuts or Spinach

**Method**

1. Lard the sweetbreads with tongue and truffles.

2. Braise them.

3. Cook the chestnuts till soft or if using spinach, cook the washed leaves on a low heat in a covered pan for 5 minutes till soft.

4. Make a puree of the cooked chestnuts or spinach by passing them through a wire sieve.

5. Dish the sweetbreads up on a bed of chestnut or spinach puree.

# Ris de Veau Buttoe

## (Calf Sweetbreads)

Calf sweetbreads
Egg
Breadcrumbs
Mushrooms

**Method**

1. Braise the sweetbreads and when cold, cut in slices.

2. Dip each slice in egg and breadcrumbs and fry.

3. Use the braising juices to make a good sauce flavoured with mushrooms.

4. Pour the sauce over the sweetbreads.

# Ris de Veau Imperatrice

## (Calf Sweetbreads Empress style)

Calf sweetbreads
Lard
Forcemeat
(made with minced chicken, cream, chopped onion, chopped herbs, and bound together with a beaten egg)
Macaroni (cooked al dente)

### Method

1. Lard the sweetbreads and braise them.

2. Make the forcemeat and shape it into balls and bake them.

3. When cool, arrange them in a border around the edge of a serving dish. Place cooked macaroni at each end.

# Supreme de Poulet Norvegienne

1 Chicken
8 oz Rice
2 Tomatoes
1 Leaf Gelatine
1 teaspoon Grated Horseradish
½ pt Whipped cream
Consommé
Truffle and tongue to garnish

### Method

1. Braise a chicken. When cold, cut as many fillets as possible from it.

2. Have a good sauce made from the liquor in which put a leaf of gelatine. When nearly cold, pour carefully over the fillets.

3. When properly set, they can be trimmed round and a garnish made by cooking a little rice in consommé.

4. After it is cold, add a little horseradish, two tomatoes in dice and a little whipped cream. Season to taste and put in a stew pan to freeze.

5. Turn out frozen rice on to platter and arrange chicken cutlets around it.

6. The cutlets can be decorated with cut truffle and tongue.

# Supreme de Faisan St Hubert

Pheasant(s)
Butter for frying
Fresh tomatoes (made into a puree)
French plums (lightly stewed)
Quenelles of pheasant
St Hubert Sauce (a barbecue sauce of Canadian origin)

**Method**

1. Fillet the pheasant(s).

2. Make the quenelles: mince pheasant meat from the legs, seasoning it and mixing it to a stiff paste with egg white.

3. Roll portions of the mixture on a floured surface to form into dumplings fry gently on all sides in butter. Keep them warm.

4. Cook the fillets (fry gently in butter).

5. Mask them with tomato puree.

6. Dish on a border and between each fillet, put a small quenelle of pheasant.

7. Arrange French Plums in the centre.

8. Serve with St Hubert's Sauce.

# Talmouse aux Huitres

1 or 2 dozen oysters
1 dessertspoon curry paste
1 oz butter
1 oz flour
1 pint water
pastry (made with 8oz flour, 4oz butter)

**Method**

1. Blanch the oysters, strain and reserve the liquor and mince them small.

2. Make some white sauce with the liquor and if preferred, a spoonful of curry paste.

3. When cold, have ready some pastry. Roll it out, cut out circles and put a spoonful of the oyster mixture in the centre of each one.

4. Press edges of pastry together into three cornered shapes and fry.

5. Serve very hot with parsley.

# Tournedos a la Parisienne

*Filet of Beef*

*Foiegras*

*Aspic*

*Brown Sauce*

*Salad de Legumes*

**Method**

1. Cook the fillet of beef and allow it to cool.

2. Cut the cold beef into thin slices.

3. Cut the same size of slices of foiegras.

4. Put the foiegras in the centre of the slices of beef.

5. Cover with brown sauce.

6. Serve cold with aspic and salad de legumes (vegetable salad).

# VEGETABLE DISHES

# Fonds d'Artichauts a la Mornay

Artichoke hearts warmed in water and filled with buttered eggs with parmesan in the eggs.

# Fonds d'Artichauts Farcie

Artichoke hearts (prepared for stuffing)

Minced chicken

Forcemeat

Butter

White Sauce

**Method**

1. Stuff the bottom of the artichoke with minced chicken.

2. Put a layer of forcemeat on top.

3. Put on a buttered sauté pan and cook in the oven (about 180°c. for 30 minutes).

4. Make a white sauce and serve with it.

# Lady Cavendish's Cabbage Pudding

**Method**

1. Blanch a few of the best leaves of a good savoury cabbage keeping them a good colour.

2. Well cook the remainder of the cabbage.

3. Chop it up, adding seasoning and cream and 1 egg.

4. Spread out the leaves making them meet.

5. Pour in the chopped cabbage and fold over the leaves to make it look like a white cabbage.

6. Wrap it in wax paper and poach in the oven till the centre is firm.

# Salade d'Orange

*(very good served instead of vegetables with duck)*

*3-4 Oranges*
*1 teaspoon vinegar*
*1 oz oil*
*3 tablespoons brandy*
*A little Maraschino*
*A pinch of sugar*

**Method**

1. Cut the oranges the same as for compotes.

2. Sprinkle on a little chopped tarragon.

3. Mix up the other ingredients and pour it over the oranges.

# Tomatoes a la St Germain

*Tomatoes of an even size and good shape*
*Brown breadcrumbs*
*Minced cooked chicken or brawn*
*Croutons*

**Method**

1. Remove cores from tomatoes.

2. Fill with minced chicken or brawn.

3. Put brown breadcrumbs on top.

4. Bake for 10 minutes (at 180°c.).

5. Serve up on croutons.

# Vegetable Marrow Fried

**Method**

1. Trim the marrow and cut it up like potato straws.

2. Sprinkle with salt to get the water out.

3. Squeeze well in a rubber.

4. Flour it well and fry it a nice golden brown.

# PUDDINGS

# Abricot Creme

*4 egg whites*

*1 spoonful apricot Jam*

*Rind of 1 lemon*

*Juice of 2 lemons*

*Sugar to taste*

**Method**

1. Chop lemon rind very fine.

2. Whip egg white in the egg bowl.

3. Whip jam and lemon rind into the egg white.

4. Add lemon juice and sugar to taste.

# Abricots a l'Armoricaine

*French roll (baguette)*

*Icing Sugar*

*Vegetable oil*

*Fresh apricots*

**Method**

1. Blanch apricots by pouring boiling water over them and then draining them and plunging them in cold water so skins easily peel off. Cut each one in half.

2. Slice bread into ½ inch thick rounds and fry these croutons.

3. Glacee with the icing sugar and place half apricot cut side down on each one.

4. Serve with a custard sauce.

# Alexandra Charlotte

Sponge fingers (see separate recipe)

¼ lb grated chocolate

½ pint milk

Sugar to taste

8 sheets gelatine

2 yolks of eggs

½ pint double cream

Vanilla or maraschino flavouring

Apricot sauce

Pistachio nuts

## Method

1. Line a plain mould with sponge fingers.

2. Gently heat milk with chocolate in it until melted.

3. Sweeten to taste and then mix in the gelatine till dissolved.

4. Lightly beat 2 egg yolks and mix into the chocolate mixture till completely blended.

5. Allow to cool. Meanwhile, stiffly whip the double cream.

6 Add vanilla or maraschino flavouring to the cooled chocolate mixture.

7. Fold in the whipped cream.

8. When mixed, pour into mould.

9. Serve with apricot sauce and pistachio nuts.

# Baba au Rhum

½ lb flour  ½ pt loaf sugar
4 eggs  1 pt water
½ oz yeast  ½ glass rum
2 oz butter
2 oz raisins
2 oz currants
2 oz sultanas
A little warm milk

**Method**

1. Dissolve the yeast in warm milk and a pinch of sugar.

2. Add to it the flour and eggs and knead it all well together.

3. Put in a warm place for an hour.

4. Mix fruit, butter and a little pinch of salt.

5. Have the moulds well buttered. Put the mixture into them and let it well rise.

6. Bake them in a quick oven (200°c.) for 20 minutes.

7. Prepare a syrup: dissolve ½ pt loaf sugar into a pint of water. Let it boil then add half a glass of rum.

8. Un-mould the babas onto serving dishes and pour over the rum syrup.

# Bakewell Pudding

8 oz (short crust or rough puff) pastry
2 oz fresh butter
6 eggs
6 oz fine sugar
½ wineglass brandy
A few bitter almonds and a few sweet almonds

**Method**

1. Line a pie dish with some pastry.

2. Melt the butter and mix it with 6 egg yolks, sugar and brandy.

3. Beat 3 of the egg whites well, and mix with other ingredients.

4. Put the mixture into the pastry and sprinkle some almonds on top.

5. Bake in a moderate oven (160°c.).

# Caramel Pudding

3 tablespoons of sugar water

3 eggs

½ pint milk

## Method

1. Boil the sugar water into a caramel.

2. Pour this into a greased heatproof mould.

3. Beat the eggs lightly, then add the milk and beat together well.

4. Pour the mixture onto the caramel in the dish.

5. Steam for ¾ hour.

# Chocolate Cake

½ lb fresh butter

7 eggs

4 ozs flour

3 ozs pounded almonds (ground almonds)

½ lb chocolate manier grated and heated in the oven

1 teaspoonful sal volatile. (ammonium carbonate: an old form of baking powder)

## Method

1. Beat ½ lb fresh butter

2. Separate egg yolks from whites and beat separately

3. Add egg yolks and flour alternately to butter .

4. Mix in melted chocolate and fold in egg whites

5. Last of all add sal volatile. (so raising does not start too early before baking is in oven)

6. Bake in a slow oven (160°c.) for 1½ to 2 hours.

# Chocolate Pudding

3 eggs
3 oz butter
4 oz breadcrumbs
3 oz sugar
4 oz grated chocolate
½ pint milk

### Method

1. Cream butter and sugar together till light and fluffy.

2. Mix breadcrumbs into the creamed mixture alternately with the lightly beaten eggs.

3. Add the grated chocolate.

4. Stir in the milk.

5. Pour the mixture into a greased mould.

6. Steam for 1 ½ hours.

7. Serve with a custard sauce.


# Constantine Pudding

5 Penny Sponge Cakes
(now marketed as Trifle Sponges)
2 Tablespoons Creme de Riz
½ pint milk
3 oranges
1 lemon
½ teaspoon vanilla (essence)
4 eggs
Crystallised cherries

### Method

1. Put the sponge cake through a wire sieve.

2. Put the crème de riz to boil in the milk for 5 minutes.

3. Then pour over the cake crumbs.

4. Add the juice of 2 oranges and the rind of 3 also the lemon, vanilla and egg yolks.

5. Whip the whites of the eggs, add slowly.

6. Garnish mould bottom with crystallised cherries and pour on the mixture. Steam for 1¼ hours.

7. Unmould and serve with apricot sauce flavoured with Silver Tays rum. Colour with carmine.

# Creme au Cafe en Surprise

½ pint strong coffee

½ pint cream

½ pint milk

2 oz sugar

12 sheets gelatine

Sponge cake soaked in brandy

6 egg whites whipped into a stiff meringue

Puree of 8oz fresh or soaked dried apricots

**Method**

1. Mix cold coffee with milk and dissolve gelatine and sugar in it.

2. Whip cream till stiff and fold in coffee mixture.

3. Pour into bomb mould and freeze.

4. Scoop out the centre and fill with brandy-soaked sponge.

5. Turn moulded bombe out onto plate.

6. Cover with stiffly whipped meringue and salamander over.
   (modern method would be to use a kitchen blow torch)

7. Serve with hot puree of apricots or surrounded with sliced peach wedges.

# Creme Brulee
## ( Lady Cavendish Receipt )

**Method**

1. Put a pint of cream in a stewpan and let it boil a minute.

2. Put 4 yolks of eggs into a basin then add cream gradually.

3. Mix slowly. Return it to stew pan. Stir over the fire till it thickens.

4. Put into a dish. Let it get cold to form a surface. Then put a thick layer of caster sugar and return

   to the oven for a minute or two.

5. Finish by glazing top with Salamander.
   (modern method would be to use a kitchen blow torch to brulee)

# Fig Pudding

¼ lb figs
¼ lb suet
¼ lb brown breadcrumbs
3 eggs
¼ lb sugar

**Method**

1. Chop the figs.

2. Mix them together with all the other ingredients.

3. Put into a greased mould.

4. Cover with securely tied greaseproof paper.

5. Steam for 3 hours.

6. Serve with a custard sauce.

# Frangipan

½ lb castor sugar
2 oz flour
2 whole eggs
Yolks of 5 eggs
1 pint milk
Salt
Almond essence
2 oz crushed dry macaroons
3 oz butter

**Method**

1. Mix together the eggs, yolks, and sugar in a bowl.

2. Then gradually add the flour and beat till smooth.

3. Boil the milk and pour it on the mixture, stirring all the time.

4. Add a grain of salt and essence to taste.

5. Pour the mixture into a pan over a low heat and stir until it boils for a few minutes.

6. Pour mixture into a bowl and mix in the butter and crushed macaroons.

7. Transfer the frangipan to a serving dish and smooth over the surface with a buttered spoon to prevent a crust from forming.

# Ginger Pudding

3 oz flour

1 dessert spoon ginger (dried)

3oz breadcrumbs

4 oz suet

¼ lb treacle

2 oz mixed peel

½ teaspoon bicarbonate of soda

a little milk

**Method**

1. Mix all ingredients well together.

2. Put into greased mould.

3. Cover with securely tied on greaseproof paper.

4. Steam for 2½ hours.


# Half Pay Pudding

½ lb suet

½ lb currants

½ lb raisins

½ lb flour

½ lb breadcrumbs

4 tablespoons treacle

1 pint milk

**Method**

1. Mix up the ingredients well together.

2. Place mixture in a greased mould.

3. Cover with securely tied on greaseproof paper.

4. Boil for 3 hours or steam pudding.

# Louisa Pudding

6 sponge cakes

3 eggs

2 tablespoons sugar

A little milk flavoured with vanilla

## Method

1. Break sponge cakes into a mould.

2. Beat eggs and milk together well.

3. Add sugar and beat it in.

4. Pour liquid over sponge cake in mould,

5. Steam for 1 hour.

6. Serve with whipped cream (pink).


# Manchester Pudding

2 eggs

2 oz sugar

2 oz butter

3 tablespoons flour

1 teaspoon baking powder

8 oz Short crust pastry

Jam

## Method

1. Make the short crust pastry and line a pie dish with it.

2. Put a layer of jam in the bottom of the pastry lining.

3. Mix up all the other ingredients with a wooden spoon

4. Pour them on top of the jam

5. Bake at 180°c. for 20-30 minutes until done.

# Mousse a l'Ananas

*1 tin pineapple*

*½ pint cream*

*8 leaves of gelatine*

## Method

1. Strain and reserve the syrup from the tin of pineapple and cut some of the flesh into dice.

2. Pound the remainder of the pineapple in a mortar.

3. Pass it through a sieve with some of the syrup.

4. Whip some cream.

5. Melt the gelatine and work it in with the mashed pineapple.

6. Whip in the egg bowl.

7. When it comes thick, put in the whipped cream, then the diced pineapple.

8. Dish up and chill before serving.

# Marchioness of Winchester's
# Christmas Pudding
## (Mrs Hughes' Receipt)

2 lbs raisins

2 lbs sultanas

1 ½ lbs currants

2 lbs sugar

2 lbs flour

1 lb chopped almonds

1 lb chopped mixed peel

2 lbs shredded suet

2 lbs breadcrumbs

4 lemons

12 eggs

1 glass brandy

1 glass cherry brandy

2 glasses beer

2 dessertspoons spice

### Method

1. Sieve flour and spice together in large basin.

2. Mix in the other dry ingredients well.

3. Add the lightly beaten eggs, the grated rind of the lemons, the strained juice, the brandy and beer.

4. Put into greased pudding basin

   (or tie in pudding cloth and place on a plate or trivet above water level).

5. Steam for 12 hours.

# Parfait au Cafe Glacee

2 eggs

1 tablespoon castor sugar

⅕ pint strong coffee

½ pint double cream

## Method

1. Whisk together the coffee, eggs and sugar in a bowl over a pan of boiling water till it thickens.

2. Then remove the bowl from the heat and continue whisking till it is cold.

3. Whip the cream stiff and fold into the coffee mixture.

4. Freeze.

# Pouding a l'Ambois

½ lb breadcrumbs

½ lb sugar

¼ lb butter

4 eggs

Spice

1 pot marmalade

Lemon peel

**For the sauce:**

¼ lb butter

2 oz sugar

2 oz bitter almonds (ground)

1 glass brandy

## Method

1. Mix all pudding ingredients.

2. Place in pudding basin and boil for 3 hours.

3. Make the sauce by beating the ingredients to a cream near to the heat.

# Pouding a la Montmorency

½ pint milk
2 oz sugar
1 vanilla pod
2 oz ground rice mixed with ⅛ pint cold milk
2 oz warmed butter
1 oz crushed ratafia biscuits
3 egg whites
Shredded almonds
Dessicated coconut

## Method

1. Bring milk to boil with dissolved sugar and vanilla pod.

2. Mix in the rice and stir until it boils.

3. Add the warmed butter, biscuit crumbs and egg yolks.

4. Whip the whites stiffly and fold into mixture.

5. Wet mould before pouring mixture into it.

6. Steam for 1¼ hours.

7. Turn out moulded pudding onto serving dish.

8. Sprinkle with shredded almonds and dessicated coconut.

9. Serve with compote de cerises. (cherry sauce).

# Pouding au Chocolat

1 pt milk (boiled)
3 oz chocolate
1 oz sugar
7 egg yolks
3 egg whites

## Method

1. Dissolve chocolate in boiled milk.

2. Add the well beaten yolks and whipped egg whites.

3. Pour into a buttered mould.

4. Steam carefully till done.

# Pouding au Sarea Venia

*3 oz breadcrumbs*

*1 oz cake*

*2 oz bars chocolate*

*2 oz butter*

*2 oz sugar*

*4 eggs*

### Method

1. Cream butter and sugar together in a basin.

2. Melt chocolate and allow to cool slightly.

3. Stir egg yolks into melted chocolate.

4. Add chocolate to creamed sugar and butter and mix well.

5. Add breadcrumbs and crumbled cake and mix well.

6. Whip egg whites and fold into chocolate mixture.

7. Place in greased mould .

8. Steam for 1¼ hrs.

# Pouding aux Marrons

*12 oz pounded chestnuts*

*3 oz sugar*

*4 oz butter*

*A little milk*

### Method

1. Mix all the ingredients in a saucepan and slowly bring to the boil stirring.

2. (Pour into a prepared tin).

3. Bake for ¾ hour (at 160°c.).

4. Serve with apricot sauce.

# Pouding Daumoise

3 eggs

3 lemons

3 oz castor sugar

3 oz butter

½ pint cream

## Method

1. Put sugar, butter and lemon juice into a stew pan and let it dissolve.

2. Then add the yolks. Thicken it (whisking over hot water).

3. Then whip the whites (and mix together with yolk mixture).

4. Pour into prepared mould.

5. Steam.

6. Serve with whipped cream.

# Pouding Electric Light

Water ice of desired flavour

Ice cream of different colours

Night light

Maiden hair Fern

## Method

1. Make a water ice and freeze it in two round moulds.

2. Be sure and freeze it hard.

3. Pierce a hole in the centre with red hot (skewer).

4. Making it large enough to place a night light in.

5. Freeze ice cream of different colours.

6. Cut in squares and place round the night light.

7. Decorate with Maiden Hair Fern.

# Pouding Gingembre

4 oz breadcrumbs
4 oz preserved ginger, chopped
4 oz castor sugar
4 oz butter
2 eggs
½ pt boiled milk

**Method**

1. Soak the crumbs in the boiled milk.

2. Beat butter and sugar, (then add to milk and crumbs).

3. Add ginger and eggs (beaten)

4. (Pour into greased mould ) .

5. Steam for 2 hours.

# Pouding Grand Belle

3 eggs
1 pint milk
2 oz sugar
Butter
Brown breadcrumbs
Pistachio nuts

**Method**

1. Butter some dariol moulds.

2. Garnish with pistachio nuts and partly fill them with breadcrumbs.

3. Make custard with 3 eggs, milk and sugar.

4. Fill up moulds.

5. Steam.

6. Serve with compote de pommes or apple puree around.

# Pouding Louise

*A very rich custard made with cream flavoured with wine, dried fruits and crumbled ratafias, set with 4 sheets of gelatine to the mould.*

# Pouding Marquise

1 pint custard (made with 1 pint milk, 3 eggs, 2 oz sugar)

2 sheets gelatine

Puree of chestnuts

½ pint cream

## Method

1. Line a plain mould with rich custard.

2. In the centre, set a rich cream mixed with puree of chestnuts set with 2 sheets of gelatine.

# Riz au Sultan

1 pint jelly liquid

1 pint egg custard (using 1 pt milk, 1 egg, 2 oz sugar )

2 or 3 leaves of gelatine

Boiled rice (short grain or "pudding" rice)

### For the sauce:-

maraschino, 2 oz sugar,1 oz arrowroot ½ pt water

## Method

1. Take a round mould, put in some jelly and allow it to set.

2. Then put in a custard with 2 or 3 leaves of gelatine.

3. Mix the remainder of custard with the rice and pour into mould.

4. Allow to set. Turn out onto serving plate.

5. Make a sweet sauce flavoured with maraschino and pour it around the pudding.

# Timbale a la Celestine

1 Bottle of peaches (tinned or fresh could be substituted)

Carmine colouring (cochineal)

Lemon Jelly

Liqueur (Lemon or Peach Liqueur)

Pistachio nuts

## Method

1. Cut the drained peaches into a nice shape the size of the stone.

2. Lay them out on a cloth and colour each piece where the stone touched with carmine.

3. Make up lemon jelly and flavour to taste with liqueur.

4. Line a fancy mould with about an eighth of an inch thick lemon jelly and set slices of peaches all the way round the mould.

5. When the inside of the mould is covered with the fruit, fill it up with more peaches and jelly until the mould is full.

6. Put it to set.

7. When set, turn out onto a dish and pipe cream coloured with carmine in centre.

8. Sprinkle with chopped pistachio nuts.

# CAKES

# Rich Plum Cake
## (Lady Dudley's Receipt)

1 ¼ lb butter

1 ¼ lb sugar

1 ½ lb flour

1 ½ lb currants

1 ½ lb raisins

1 ½ lb sultanas

1 lb dried cherries

12-14 eggs

1 large wineglass brandy

### Method

1. Cream butter and sugar together till fluffy.

2. Add beaten eggs little by little alternately with flour.

3. Mix in the dried fruit and brandy.

4. Bake for 3 hours in a moderate oven (160°c.).

### Almond Icing

1 ½ lb ground almonds

3 lbs icing sugar

6-8 eggs (separated)

### Method

Make a stiff paste with the sugar, almonds and egg yolks and roll out to ¼ inch thick. Cut out a circle to cover cake top and re roll remainder into a rectangle to cover sides, using apricot jam to stick it to cake.

### White Sugar Icing

3 lbs icing sugar

1 lemon

### Method

Work sugar to a creamy paste with whites of eggs and lemon juice. Spread over the cake and ornament as you please.

# Chocolate Cake

½ lb fresh butter

7 eggs

4 ozs flour

3 ozs pounded almonds (ground almonds)

½ lb chocolate manier grated and heated in the oven

1 teaspoonful sal volatile.[†]

[†](ammonium carbonate: an old form of baking powder)

## Method

1. (Preheat oven to 160°c.).

2. Beat ½ lb fresh butter.

3. Separate egg yolks from whites and beat separately.

4. Add egg yolks and flour alternately to butter.

5. Mix in melted chocolate and fold in egg whites.

6. Last of all add sal volatile. (so raising does not start too early before baking is in oven)

7. Bake in a slow oven for 1½ to 2 hours.

# Genoa Cake

10 oz flour

8 oz sugar

8 oz butter

3 oz candied peel

1 oz pistachio kernels

2 oz almonds

6 oz sultanas

1 teaspoon baking powder

5 eggs

Grated rind of 1 lemon

## Method

1. (Preheat oven to 180°c.).

2. Cream sugar and butter together well.

3. Sieve flour and baking powder together.

4. Add beaten eggs and flour alternately to creamed mixture.

5. Stir in peel, rind of lemon, sultanas, chopped pistachio and almonds.

6. Put into greased cake mould lined with greaseproof paper.

7. Bake for 1½ hours in a moderate oven.

# Gulekage

3 lbs flour
½ lb butter
½ lb castor sugar
2 pints milk
½ lb mixed peel
2 handfuls sultanas
4 yolks of eggs
1 white of egg
4 or 5 tablespoons yeast

## Method

1. Mix the yeast with a little lukewarm milk.

2. Add a little flour to it till it is thick as a good white sauce.

3. Whip the yolks and white of egg together.

4. Melt the butter in the milk with the sugar in a large stew pan till it is lukewarm.

5. Add the whipped eggs, then stir the flour into the mixture.

6. Gradually add the yeast.

7. Leave the paste to rise in a warm place.

8. Butter a pan and bake in a moderate oven (180°c.).

# Honey Cake

½ breakfast cup of sugar
1 breakfast cup sour cream
2 breakfast cups flour
½ teaspoon carbonate of soda (bicarbonate of soda)
Honey to taste

## Method

1. Mix all the dry ingredients together.

2. Add the cream and honey and beat till smooth.

3. Pour into greased cake pan (or muffin moulds).

4. Bake in preheated oven at (180°c.) for 30 minutes (15 minutes if muffin moulds) till done.

5. Serve warm.

# Italian Chocolate Cake

½ lb grated chocolate
6 ozs caster sugar
½ lb butter
3 ozs potato flour
3 ozs best flour
7 eggs (6 whites and 7 yolks)

### Method

1. Beat butter and sugar together

2. Melt chocolate and cool slightly before mixing in egg yolks

3. Add flour and chocolate alternately.

4. Whip egg whites then fold into mixture.

5. Divide mixture between 4 small tins.

6. Bake in a moderate oven (180°c.). Allow to cool.

7. Make icing by boiling ½ lb sugar dissolved in water to make a syrup.

8. Then melt ½ lb chocolate and add to syrup.

9. Pour it over the cold cakes.

# Langues de Chat
## (cat's tongues)

3 whites
5 oz sugar
4 oz butter
4 ½ oz finest flour

### Method

1. Whip egg whites stiff.

2. Stir in sugar.

3. Stir in melted butter.

4. Then stir in sieved flour.

5. Spread spoonful of mixture into long tongue-shaped biscuit on greaseproof paper on baking sheet.

6. Repeat to make others leaving space between each for expansion.

7. Bake in oven at (160°c.) for 10 minutes.

# Macaroons

½ lb sweet almonds
½ lb sugar
6 oz butter
4 eggs
Wafer paper (rice paper?)
Orange water

## Method

1. Pound almonds with orange water.

2. Add sugar and egg whites beaten to a stiff froth.

3. Mix all well together and when paste looks soft, drop equal sized dollops an equal distance apart on wafer paper on a baking sheet.

4. Bake in a slow oven (140°c.).

# Shooting Cake

3 lbs flour
1 ½ lbs currants
1 ½ lbs raisins
1 ½ lbs brown sugar
1 ¾ lbs butter
½ lb mixed peel
1 nutmeg
2 teaspoons baking powder
1 teaspoon carbonate of soda (bicarb)
7 eggs

## Method

1. Cream sugar and butter until light and fluffy.

2. Sieve together the flour, bicarbonate of soda and baking powder.

3. Add a little of the beaten eggs and some of the sieved flour alternately to creamed mixture until all is incorporated.

4. Grate the nutmeg into the mixture and mix in all the dried fruit.

5. Pour mixture into a greased lined cake pan and bake in a moderate oven (180°c.) for 3 hours.

# Snow Cake

*½ lb arrowroot*

*¼ lb sugar*

*¼lb butter*

*3 eggs*

*Flavouring  (vanilla essence?)*

## Method

1.  Beat the butter to a cream.

2.  Stir in the sugar and arrowroot beating all the time.

3.  Beat in the flavouring.

4.  Whisk the egg whites till stiff, then beat the egg whites into the creamed sugar for 20 minutes.

5.  Put into greased patty pans and bake in a preheated moderate oven (180°c.) for 15 minutes.


# Sponge Fingers

*3 eggs (whites of 3, yolks of 2)*

*2 oz sugar*

*1 ½ oz flour*

## Method

1.  Preheat oven (180°c.).

2.  Beat sugar and eggs over boiling water till blood heat then beat till cold (time ¾ hour).

3.  Fold in sieved flour gradually.

4.  Pipe sponge mix in uniform finger lengths onto greased baking sheet.

5.  Bake for 10 minutes.

6.  Allow to cool before removing from tray with palette knife.

# White Mountain Cake

2 eggs

2 oz butter

2 oz sugar

2 oz flour

Teaspoon bicarbonate of soda

Teaspoon cream of tartar

**Method**

1. Sieve flour.

2. Beat the butter to a cream with the sugar.

3. Add the flour and beaten egg alternately till well mixed.

4. Mix bicarbonate and cream of tartar with a little milk and beat it into the mixture.

5. Have ready six buttered enamel plates.

6. Put enough of the mixture to cover the bottom of each plate.

7. Bake for 10 minutes (at 180°c.)

8. Have ready some icing. Put a layer of icing between each as soon as they come from the oven and cover all with icing (Can be done with any icing).

# BISCUITS

# Bread Rusks for Tea

6 oz butter

¾ lb sifted sugar

¾ lb breadcrumbs which have been baked

6 eggs

½ gill double cream

## Method

1. Stir the butter to a cream with a wooden spoon.

2. Cream in the sugar.

3. Stir in the baked breadcrumbs and the eggs 2 at a time.

4. Stir in the double cream.

5. Spread the mixture rather thickly on a (well greased) baking sheet.

6. Bake in a moderate oven (160°c.).

7. Cut into fingers and make crisp.

# Ginger Wafers

3 oz fresh butter

2 oz raw sugar

1 tablespoon ground ginger

1 teaspoon flour

## Method

1. Melt butter and sugar together on gentle heat.

2. Stir in dry ingredients and mix well.

3. Drop mixture in spoonfuls to spread thinly on to a well greased baking sheet.

4. Bake in a quick oven (180°c.) for a few minutes (5-10 minutes).

5. Serve with vanilla cream or ice cream.

# Mount Blaisy Ginger Nuts

1 lb flour

½ lb (golden) syrup

¼ lb butter

2 oz ground ginger

¼ lb sugar

Milk

**Method**

1. Rub butter into (sieved) flour and ginger.

2. Mix in sugar and syrup.

3. Moisten with milk.

4. Drop mixture on to well greased baking sheet.

5. Bake (160°c.) 20 minutes.


# Plain Ginger Nuts

1 lb flour

½ lb butter

1 oz ground ginger

¼ lb sugar

¾ lb golden syrup

**Method**

1. Mix all into a stiff paste with about ¾ lb golden syrup.

2. Roll into biscuits.

3. Bake in a moderate oven (160°c.).

# Tea Biscuits

¼ lb butter

¼ lb flour

1 oz fine sugar

1 egg

## Method

1. Rub the butter, sugar, flour together.

2. Add the yolk of the egg. Work it into a paste.

3. Roll our very thin.

4. Cut out with a fluted cutter.

5. Bake in a gentle oven (160°c.).


# Wafer Gingerbread

½ lb flour

½ lb sugar

½ lb butter

½ lb treacle

1 teaspoon powdered ginger

## Method

1. Rub the butter and flour together.

2. Add the sugar and ginger.

3. Put in the treacle and mix to a stiff batter.

4. Drop spoonfuls of mixture onto a well greased baking sheet and bake in a hot oven (180°c.) for 5 – 10 minutes.

5. (While still warm), roll round the handle of a wooden spoon to make into a curled finger shape.

68

# PRESERVES

# Cherry Jam

12 lbs cherries (or less)

¾ lb sugar to every lb cherries

**Method**

1.  Put (stoned) cherries in a preserving pan with sugar.

2.  Boil up quickly for about ¾ hour.

3.  Put kernels (tied in a muslin bag) in a few minutes before it is done.

4.  When it sets, remove kernels and bottle jam in dry sterilised jars.


# Crab Apple Jelly

Crab Apples

Sugar (allow 1lb for every pint of juice)

Water

**Method**

1.  Boil crabs in water until they break.

2.  Pass them through a jelly bag.

3.  Measure the juice collected and place in pan with 1 lb sugar to each pint of juice.

4.  Boil quickly until it jellies.

5.  Bottle in dry sterilised jars.

(It should be clear and red. This is good for whooping cough).

# Marmalade

12 Oranges

2 lemons

3 sweet oranges

Sugar  (1 lb for every lb of fruit)

**Method**

1.  Divide the fruit into quarters.

2.  Take away all the seeds.

3.  Cut the rind in very small slices.

4.  Put the seeds in to soak (in a small muslin bag) for 12 hours.

5.  Then weigh it.

6.  Into a basin put 1 pt water for every lb fruit.

7.  Stand for 24 hours, then boil it until tender.

8.  Stand for 24 hours and weigh it. Remove seeds.

9.  Put it onto a fire allowing 1 lb sugar to each lb fruit.

10. Boil briskly till it jellies. Then bottle it.

# Marrow Jam

10 lb marrow cut into chunks

¾ lb sugar to each lb marrow

2 oz ginger

Rind of 2 lemons cut very fine

**Method**

1.  About half fill the preserving pan with water and put in the marrow.

2.  Boil it till tender.

3.  Add the sugar, lemon rind and ginger and boil it till it sets.

4.  Bottle it in dry sterilised jars.

71

# Mincemeat

## (Miss Bullen's Receipt)

1 lb Chopped Suet

1 lb stoned raisins

1 lb dried currants

1 lb dried sultanas

2 nutmegs

6 apples

4 lemons

½ pint brandy

**Method**

1. Put all this into a basin. Mix well up.

2. Add the lemon juice and brandy last.

3. Put it into (dry sterilised) jars and tie down 6 weeks before Christmas.

# Rowanberry Jelly

Ripe red Rowan berries (weighed)

½ pint water to every 2lbs fruit

1 lb sugar to every 1 pint of juice

**Method**

1. Put the berries in a preserving pan with the water.

2. Simmer, breaking the berries with a spoon to make the juice flow freely.

3. When they are quite soft and well broken, put into a jelly bag.

4. Run off in the usual way and catch the juice.

5. Put it back in the pan with 1 lb sugar to each pint of juice.

6. Boil till it jellies.

7. Bottle in dry sterile jars.

# DRINKS

# Cherry Brandy

Round, ripe Morello cherries weighed

For every pound of fruit:

3 oz crushed sugar candy

10 cherry kernels

2 cloves

Good brandy

## Method

1. Half fill some wide-mouthed sterilised bottles with cherries.

2. Add the kernels, cloves and sugar candy and fill up with good brandy.

3. Cork and seal securely and leave it for 3 months.

4. Then strain and rebottle it.

# Elderberry Wine

To make 1 gallon wine:

1 ½ pints syrup (juice of the elderberries)

3 lb loaf sugar

2 oz ginger well smashed

½ lb raisins well smashed

1 lemon

## Method

1. Mash the elderberries and pass them through a muslin strainer.

2. Collect the syrup and measure it.

3. Peel the lemon and smash the ginger.

4. Put them into the syrup with the sugar and boil for half an hour.

5. Well skim it while boiling.

6. Pour it into a pan over the raisins and lemon flesh.

7. When new milk-warm, it should be worked with a little yeast on a little toast for the night.

8. Strain it all into dry, sterilised bottles and well cork it down.

# Ginger Beer

2 oz cream of tartar

2 oz whole ginger (chopped)

2lbs loaf sugar

1 lemon cut in slices

1 egg white

**Method**

1. Put the ingredients into a large pan, pour 3 gallons of boiling water on it and let it stand until it is as warm as new milk.

2. Then beat egg white and put into it also 1 oz german yeast.

3. Mix these well and cover over with a cloth.

4. Let it stand till next morning. Then take off the froth.

5. Strain it through a cloth, bottle it (in sterilised bottles) and tie the corks down.

6. It will be ready to drink in 2 days.

# Orange Gin

## (March 8th 1900)

3 Seville oranges

sugar candy

1 quart of best gin

**Method**

1. Cut the peel very thin from 3 Seville oranges.

2. Add a teacupfull of pounded sugar candy.

3. Let it stand in a china bowl 24 hours.

4. Then pour over a quart of the best gin.

5. Four hours after put all including the peel into a bottle.

6. Cork it well and let it stand for a month, then strain it through a piece of flannel to make it bright (clear) and bottle it (in sterilised bottles) and it will improve by keeping but can be used at once.

# Sloe Gin

*3 quarts pricked sloes*

*2 ½ lbs small pieces sugar candy*

*1 oz sloe kernels*

*1 gallon of unsweetened gin*

### Method

1. Into a 2 gallon jar put all the dry ingredients.

2. Pour on this 1 gallon of unsweetened gin.

3. Let the jar be well shaken 2 or 3 times a week for 3 months.

4. Clean strain and bottle it (in sterilised bottles) seal it down well.

# SAUCES

# Cumberland Sauce *(For venison)*

2 sticks of horseradish
2 oranges
2 lemons grated and the juice
A little redcurrant jelly
Caster sugar
1 tablespoon white vinegar
A little mustard
Salt according to taste
1 glass port wine

### Method

1. Clean, peel and grate horseradish.

2. Mix all ingredients thoroughly.

3. Bring ingredients to the boil in a small pan, stirring with a wooden spoon.

4. Simmer gently for 15 minutes so that it reduces by about half.

# Espagnole Sauce

¼ pt good brown sauce (brown roux  with veal stock added)
¼ oz good glaze (made by reducing brown stock)
1 fresh  mushroom
½ wineglass sherry

### Method

1. Mix the glaze, brown sauce and sherry.

2. Add sliced mushroom.

3. Boil for 15 minutes, stirring. It is then ready for use.

# Sauce Bearnaise

5 yolks of egg
5 oz butter

### Method

1. Add 1 oz of butter in small pieces to the 5 egg yolks while whipping them over a slack fire (low heat) till the yolks begin to thicken.

2. Take off the stove and add another ounce of butter.

3. Continue this process until 5 oz butter is added making a consistency of mayonnaise.

(interesting that no mention is made of adding chopped tarragon here)

# Sauce for Creme of Fish

Bones of fish from filleting

Bunch of herbs: bay leaf, thyme, parsley,

Black peppercorns

Fresh mushrooms

2 onions

½ pint white wine

Lemon juice

2 oz live spawn

2 oz fine flour

2 oz butter

## Method

1. Cover bones and spawn with cold water, wine and the lemon juice.

2. Add chopped onion and mushroom, herbs and spices.

3. Simmer for ½ hour.

4. Strain it off and (gradually) add 1 pint of this liquor to (a roux made from) the fine flour and butter.

5. Stir in ¼ pint cream. and use the sauce.

# Sauce for Wild Duck

A little salt

Cayenne

A little sugar

Juice of 1 lemon

A little ketchup

1 tablespoon Harvey Lane (sherry)

1 tablespoon of port wine

## Method

Mix up all the ingredients.

# Venison Sauce

Redcurrant jelly

Brown Sauce

A little port wine

Bay leaf

Pepper corn

Parsley

1 shallot

## Method

1. Chop a shallot very fine and put it into the vegetable pan with bay leaf, peppercorn, parsley and a glass of port wine.

2. Reduce it to glaze and then add a small quantity of redcurrant jelly and brown sauce.

3. Boil all together and jelly, then strain.

# Notes

## Notes on Soups

**Consommé a la Parisienne:**
made with Spanish onion fried, thin slices of bread parmesan cheese on the bread, consommé poured over

**Sarah Bernard:**
Tapioca quenelles, marrow cut in dice

**A L'Imperial:**
Tapioca, eggs and cream to be added last minute.

**Potage Fines Herbes:**
Lettuce, sorrel, chervil, pass in butter then through the sieve, add eggs and cream.

**Petite Marmite:**
Pieces of meat cooked in the consommé and vegetables.

**Potage St Germain:**
Made with peas, put whole peas in it.

**Potage Perlis de Nizam**
**Consommé Nelson**
**Consommé au Fromage**
**Consommé Allemande**
**Creme de Choufleur**
**Potage Laitue:**
Lettuce blanched then braised. Thin slices of bread, dried, put in the consommé.

**Creme de Riz a la Reine:**
Chicken and rice boiled in stock, pounded in the mortar.

**Croute au Pot**
**Consommé Oxtail**
**Consommé Colbert:**
Eggs poached in the consommé.

**Consommé a la fermiere**
Clear soup with only the yolks of eggs poached and put in.

## Notes on Other Dishes

**Cotelettes a la Reforme:**
Ragout in the centre, parsley in the crumbs, red currant jelly in the sauce.

**Royale for Soup**
Beat well together 2 eggs and the same quantity of stock,, with pepper and salt to taste, put into a mould to steam.

**Pain de Fruits Chantilly**
A mixture of fruit passed through a wire sieve then set with gelatine, put in a border mould. When set, turn out. Fill in the centre with vanilla cream.

**Mousse au Citron**
Whipped whites of eggs, grated rind and juice of 2 lemons  set with gelatine. Serve rich custard sauce with it.

**Souffle d'Oranges**
Half Oranges filled with cold soufflé.

81

# MENUS

# Diner du Mars 1

Potage Puree de Cressy

Peinon

Saumon sauce Genoise

Entree

Cotelettes Poycestres aux pois

Roti Salade

Chouxfleur Gratin

Meringue a la Creme

# Diner du Mars 22

❧

Potage Printanier

Peinon

Saumon sauce Genoise

Entrée

Noisettes de Mouton

Salade

Pouding Saxon

Fromage Bellvus

Savroy Roti

❧

# Diner du Mai 25

Consommé Printanier

Peinne

Noisettes de Mouton Jardinier

Boeuf braisee a la Terrine

Poulet Roti

Salade

Entrements

Pouding a l'Abricot

Cerises a la Jubilee

# Diner du Juin 1

Consommé Colbert

Truite Souchet Froid

Cailles a la Lucullus

Gigot de Mouton Roti

# Diner du Juin 3

Consommé Printanier

Filets de Sole a la Cardinale

Cotelettes d'Agneau a la Russe

Poulet Braise et Langue

Glace Pumpernickle (Brown Bread)

Croutes de Foie de Volaille au Diable

# Diner du Juin 4

⚜

Consommé au Riz

Saumon sauce Ravigot

Cotelettes de Volaille

Boef Froid

Asperges en Branches froid

Caneton Roti au Petis Pois

Cafe a la Creme Glace

Pailles au parmesan

⚜

# Diner du Juin 10

Consommé a la Royale

Filets de Sole a la Cardinale

Chaudfroid de Pigeons

Gelle d'Agneau Roti

Poulets au Cressons

Asperges en Branches

Glace en Surprise

Croute au Thon

# Diner du Juin 11

Consommé Printanier

Truite Froid Sauce Vert

Cotelettes de Volaille en Supreme

Boeuf Froid

Caneton Roti

Mousse a l'Ananas

Croute a la Marguerite

# Diner du Juin 14

Consommé au Norginere

Poisson

Fruite Souchet

Entree

Petite Lapin a la Creme

L'Agneau Froid

Asperges a l'Huile

Canapes au jambon Rapee

# Diner du Juin 15

Consommé

Poisson

Blanchailles

Entree

Cotelettes d'Agneau en Chaudfroid

Pigeons Roti au Petis Pois

Mousse au Camembert

# Diner du Juin 19

Consommé Brunoise

Mayonaise du Saumon

Timbales de Volaille a l'Aspic

Gigot d'Agneau Roti

Mousse au Peches

Les Oeufs a la Tartare

# Diner du Juin 28

Consommé au Vermiceli

Slips Frit sauce Anchoise

Entree

Ris de Veau a la Jardinere

L'Agneau froid Sauce Menthe

Legumes

Broad Beans & Bacon

Sardines a la Diable

# Diner du Juin 29

Consommé Printaniere

Poisson

Filets de sole Souchet

Entree

Cotelettes d'Agneau Grilleau Vois

Reliev

Voulet Roti au Cresson

Entrements

Omelettes Soufflie a l'Abricot

Sandwiches aux Camembert

# Diner du Juillet 3

❧

Consommé Quenelles de Volaille

Truite Froide Sauce Vert

Poulet Saute la Valliere

Gelle d'Agneau

Souffle Glace

Compote de Cerises

Pailles au Parmesan

❧

# Luncheon July 10

Cotelettes du Saumon en Aspic
Entrees
Cotelettes d'Agneau Chaudfroid

Petite filets de Boeuf au fond article

Poulets Rotis au Cresson

Salad

Viands Froid

Mousse au Langue

Boeuf Pressed

Jambon

Langue de Boeuf

Langue de Mouton
Entrements
Riz au Peches

Souffle Glace au Fraise

Gateau au Genoise

Sanwiches au Camembert

# Diner du Aug 12

‽

Consommé a la Royale

Poisson

Rissoles de Volaille

Filet de Boeuf Roti

Glace Vanille

Cerises Jubilee

Foie de Volaille au Diable

❧

# Diner du Nov 10

Potage conservative

Buisson d'eperlans tartare

Riz de veau Chevalure

Selle d'agneau

Faizans

Corbeille de poires glace

Gondoles Dinbois

# Luncheon (out) Nov 10

❧

Hot pot of Mutton

Caneton Roti

Galantine of pressed Beef

Jam Turnover

Tapioca Pudding

Stewed Plums

❧

# Diner du Nov 11

❦

Huitres aux Natural

Consommé a la Sevigna

Slip Vin Blanc

BoucheesPerigourdines

Filet de Boef Strasbourg

Poulets aux Riz

Meringues Glacee de Framboise

Croutes d'Oeufs

⁂

# Luncheon Nov 11

✦

Curried Mutton

Pheasants

Pork Pie

Plum Pudding

Crème au caramel

Gateau au Pithmain

Rice Cakes & Jam Sauce

✦

# Tuesday Nov 14

Huitres au Naturel

Consommé a la Princesse

Cotelettes de Turbot

Volaille a la Rothschild

Mousse du Jambon a l'Aspic

Filet de Boeuf a la Clairmont

Poulets Roti

Corbeilles d'Oranges Glace

Croutes a la Marlborough

*Huitres au Naturel*

*Tortue a la Reine*

*Saumon sauce Persil*

*Blanchaille*

*Pouding au Becasse*

*Ris de Veau*

*Aloyan de Boeuf*

*Agneau Roti sauce menthe*

*Dinde Bouillie sauce Celeries*

*Paunche a la Romain*

*Asperges a l'hollandaise*

*Souffle au Vanille*

*Charlotte Russe et Gelle*

*Pouding Glace Nesselrode*

*Dessert*

*Cafe*

# Samedi

Potage Belge

Pernou

Whitebait

Entree

Gigot de Mouton Braisé

Cailles Roti

Haricots Verts

Savroy

Petis Pois Paysanne

Saint Honore a la Crème

Ris de Veau a la Forrestière

Cote de Mouton a l'Indienne

Petites Carottes Vichy

Oeufs Tripe

Filets de boeuf brenoise

Souffle a l'Abricot

Compotes de groseilles

# Dimanche

❧

Potage

Pernore

Truites froide Meunière

Entree

Ris de Veau Forrestière

Quartier d'Agneau

Boeuf froide

Salade

Asperges a l'huile

Entree

Souffle Glace

Caviar

❧

# Dejeuner

Les Oeufs en Cocottes

Boeuf Roti

Cromestu de Volaille

Choux fleure gratiné

Meringue a la crème

Pouding de Riz

# Diner

❧

Consommé a la Royale

Poisson

Croquettes de Volaille

Epaule de Mouton Roti

❦

# Luncheon

❧

Lapereau sauté

Biftek Grille au Maitre d'Hotel

Souffle au Semoule

Compote de Prunes

❦

# Glossary of French Words

Some of the words in the menus are not included below because they are
place names or people who the dish has been named after.
One or two words below may have been mis-spellings by Ada of similar sounding words.

### ᔋ A ᔋ

Abricots ....................................................apricots
Agneau ..........................................................lamb
Ananas ...................................................pineapple
Anchoise ................................................anchovy
Artichaut.................................................artichoke
Asperges..................................................asparagus
Aspic .........................................clear unflavoured gelatine

### ᔋ B ᔋ

Biftek ...........................................................steak
Blanchailles ...........................................whitebait
Boeuf ...........................................................beef
Bouilli(e) ...................................................boiled
Buisson ...............little bush (*is also a place in Provence, France*)
Braisee ........................................................braised
Branches........................................spears (*as in asparagus*)

### ᔋ C ᔋ

Cailles...........................................................quail
Caneton .....................................................duckling
Cerises.........................................................cherries
Chaud-froid .....................cold, jellied (*or game with mayonnaise*)
Chouxfleur ...............................................cauliflower
Compote ........................................................stew
Consommé .......................................clear soup or broth
Corbeille ......................................................basket
Cotelettes.....................................................cutlets
Crevettes .....................................................shrimps
Croutes .......................crusts (*thin slices of baguette, toasted*)

### ᔋ D ᔋ

Diable ................devil (*au diable = devilled, by the addition of hot pepper*)
Dinde ..........................................................turkey

### ᔋ E ᔋ

Eperlans ......smelts, a sea fish of delicate flesh like salmon or trout
Epaule.......................................................shoulder

### ᔋ F ᔋ

Faisan...........................................................pheasant
Fraise ........................................................strawberry
Framboise.....................................................raspberry
Frit ........................................................fried, chips
Foie .............................................................liver
Foiegras.............................specially fattened goose liver
Fonds...................consommé or basic stock made from meat bones
seasonings and vegeta-
bles
Froid ............................................................cold
Fromage......................................................cheese

### ᔋ G ᔋ

Gateau ..............................fancy iced and decorated sponge cake
Gelle (gel) .....................................................jelly
Gigot .............................................................leg
Glace ............................................ice cream or sorbet
Gondoles .............................gondola boat-shaped pastries
Gratin ................................grated cheese topping
Groseilles ...................................................currants

### ᔋ H ᔋ

Haricots Verts ........................................green beans
Huile .............................................................oil
Huitres .......................................................oysters

### ᔋ J ᔋ

Jambon .........................................................ham

### ᔋ L ᔋ

Langue .........................................................tongue
Lapin .........................................................rabbit
Lapereau ..................................................baby rabbit
Lievre ...........................................................hare
Legumes ...................................................vegetables

### ᔋ M ᔋ

Menthe .........................................................mint
Meuniere ......................................Rolled in flour and fried in butter,
usually with lemon juice and chopped parsley sprinkled on top.
Used of fish.

Mouton ...........................................mutton or lamb

### ᔋ N ᔋ

Noisettes ...............................a small round piece of meat fillet

### ᔋ O ᔋ

Oeufs ............................................................eggs
Oeufs en Cocottes .....................eggs in individual ceramic dishes
steamed or baked.

### ᔋ P ᔋ

Pailles...........................................................straws
Paunch(e) ....................................................belly
Paysanne ....................................................peasant
Peches .........................................................peaches
Perdreau ...................................................partridge
Persil ..........................................................parsley
Petits Pois ......................................................peas
Poires ..........................................................pears
Poisson ..........................................................fish
Potage ...........................................................soup
Pouding........................................................pudding
Poulet .........................................................chicken
Peinon/Peinne .........................................penne pasta
or could be a mis-spelling of pain i.e. bread

### ᔋ Q ᔋ

Quartier .......................................................quarter
Quenelles ...................................................dumplings

### ᔋ R ᔋ

Ravigot(e) ..............vinaigrette with fine herbs, capers and shallots
Reliev ........a dish usually a bit larger than and following an entree
Riz.................................................................rice
Ris de Veau ....................................calf sweetbreads

### ᔋ S ᔋ

Saumon .......................................................salmon
Salade...........................................................salad
Sauté ........................................................pan-fried
Savroy ...............could be a misspelling of savoureux i.e. savouries
Selle .............................................................saddle
Semoule ....................................................semolina
Slips ...................................possibly some kind of fish
Souchet........................................a place in France

### ᔋ T ᔋ

Terrine ...........lidded ceramic dish for baking pâté or meat dishes.
Thon ...........................................................tuna
Tortue..........................................................turtle
Truite ...........................................................trout

### ᔋ V ᔋ

Vert ............................................................green
Viande(s) ......................................................meat
Volaille.........................................................fowl

110

# Select Bibliography

**"An English Gamekeeper"**
by John Wilkins. *Sporting and Leisure Press ISBN 0 86023 426 6*

**"Cooking For Kings: The Life of the First Celebrity Chef Anton Careme"**
by Ian Kelly, *Short Books 2003 ISBN 1-904095-93-3*

**"Country House Life Family and Servants 1815-1914"**
Jessica Gerrard. *Blackwell ISBN 0-631-15566-X*

**"Edward VII"**
Denis Judd. *Purnell 1975*

**"Keeping Their Place: Domestic Service in the Country House 1700-1920"**
Pamela A.Sambrook. *Stroud Sutton 2005 ISBN 0-7509-3559-6*

**"Life Below stairs at Gayhurst House"**
by Esther Wesley. *Transcript of recording of her talk to the Stoke Goldington Association. 1990*

**"Queen Elizabeth the Queen Mother: The Official Biography"**
by William Shawcross. *Pan Books ISBN 978-0-330-43430-0*

**"The Country House Kitchen, 1650-1900".**
Pamela A. Sambrook and Peter Brears. *2010 ISBN 01780752455969*

**"The Country House Servant"**
Pamela A. Sambrook. *Sutton. 1999 ISBN 0-7509-1632-x*

**"A Country House at Work. Three centuries of Dunham Massey"**
Pamela Sambrook. *The National Trust ISBN 0-7078-0344-6*

**"The Escoffier Cookbook and Guide to the Fine Art of Cookery"**
by Auguste Escoffier, *Crown Publishers Inc. New York 1989 ISBN 0-517-50662-9*

**"Up and Down Stairs: The History of the Country House Servant"**
Jeremy Musson. *Murray 2009 ISBN 978-0719597307*

# *Index*

*Artwork, Illustration, Design & Typesetting completed by Guy's Artworks*
*E-mail: guys.artworks@btinternet.com*

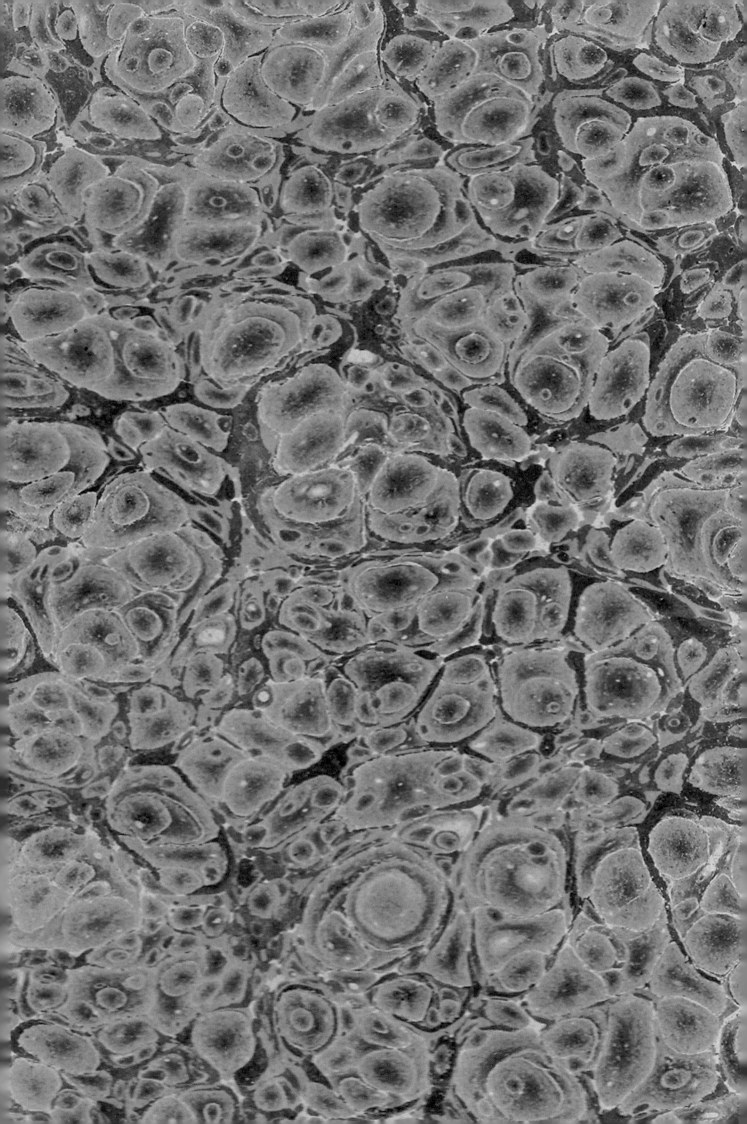